BOATOPIA

photographed
by
FRANÇOISE LEGRAND

compiled and introduced
by
GODFREY HOWARD

Hearst Marine Books
New York

Library of Congress Catalog Card Number: 85-80263

ISBN: 0-688-06163-X
Printed in Italy
   First U.S. Edition

1   2   3   4   5   6   7   8   9   10

First published in Great Britain in 1985 by Robert Royce Limited

Produced and designed by
Malcolm Saunders Publishing Ltd and Savitri Books Ltd
71 Great Russell Street
London WC1B 3BN
Great Britain

Designed by Mrinalini Srivastava

Set in Garamond by Dorchester Typesetting, Dorchester
Reproduction by Gateway Platemakers, London
Printed and bound in Italy by Arnoldo Mondadori Company.

Endpapers. The Loiret, a river in France.

For all the sailors,
fishermen and other
mariners who have
given life to this book

* * *

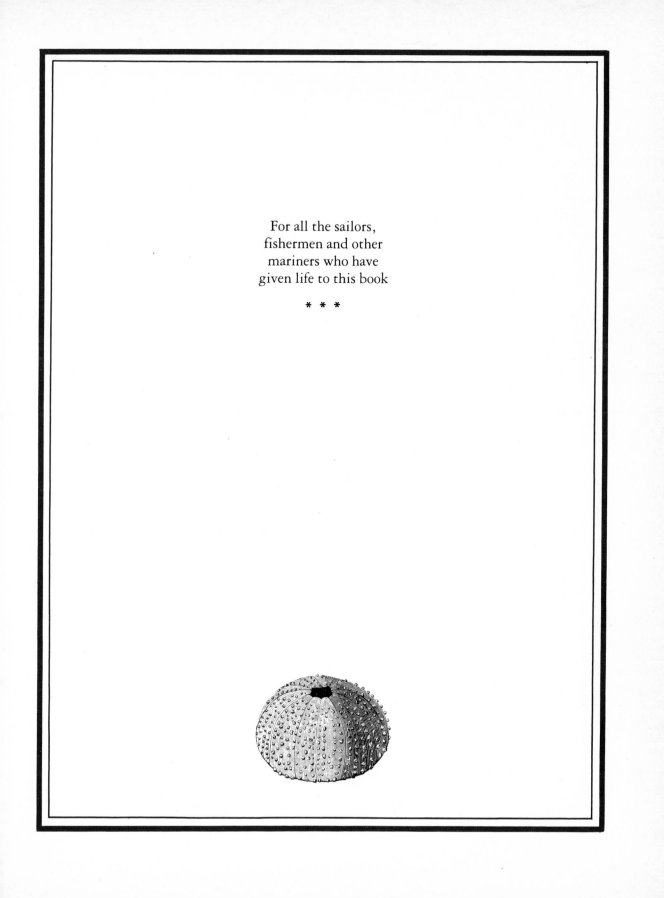

CONTENTS

ACKNOWLEDGEMENTS

We are grateful to the following publishers and others who have generously helped us to raise money for the Royal National Lifeboat Institution (direct or through the Association For Rescue At Sea, New York), by allowing us to use extracts from copyright material, without charging their usual fees. Every effort has been made to trace the owners of the copyright of all extracts used: if there are any accidental omissions or inaccuracies, please accept our apologies.
Acknowledgements to the texts are given in the order in which they appear in the book. When more than one extract from the same book appears, only one acknowledgement is given.

Chapter 1 – *The Way of a Ship*
Professor E. J. Richards, University of Southampton.
Macmillan Publishing Company, New York: *The Ancient Mariners* by Lionel Casson.
Maurice Michael: *A History of Seamanship* by Douglas Phillips-Birt.
W. W. Norton and Company, Inc.: *Seawise* by Donald M. Street, Jr. © 1979 Donald M. Street, Jr.
Hutchinson Publishing Group Limited: *Sailing* by Richard Hughes and the letter from Uffa Fox (*The Saturday Book*); *Windjammer 'Prentice* by Captain Vincent Large.
George Allen & Unwin Publishers Ltd: *'Racundra's' First Cruise* by Arthur Ransome.
John Farquharson Ltd.: *The Lonely Sea and the Sky* by Francis Chichester.
Sidgwick & Jackson: *Sailing – A Course of My Life* by Edward Heath.
David & Charles: *Women Under Sail*, edited by Basil Greenhill and Ann Giffard.
Harrap Limited: *The Seaman's World*, edited by Ronald Hope, with acknowledgements to The Marine Society and Mrs. Mark Simpson.
William Collins Sons & Co. Ltd. and Alfred A. Knopf, Inc., New York: *The Last Voyage* by Hammond Innes. Copyright Hammond Innes, 1978.
Conway Maritime Press: *Out of Appledore* by W. J. Slade.
Ministry of Defence (Navy): *Naval Ratings Handbook*, Crown Copyright.
Pelham Books Ltd.: *Come Hell or High Water* by Clare Francis.

Chapter 2 – *The Lonely Sea and the Sky*
The Society of Authors, literary representative of the Estate of John Masefield: *Sea Fever*
Macmillan Publishing Company, New York: *Sea Fever* from the *Poems of John Masefield*. Copyright John Masefield, 1953.
John Farquharson Ltd.: *Atlantic Adventure* by Francis Chichester.
Simon & Schuster, Inc.: *Britannia: Rowing Alone Across the Atlantic* by John Fairfax.
Granada Publishing Limited: *Sailing Alone Around the World* by Captain Joshua Slocum.
Martin Secker & Warburg Limited: *The Last Grain Race* by Eric Newby.
André Deutsch Ltd., and Alfred A. Knopf, Inc., New York: *Winter Ocean* from *Telephone Poles and other Poems* by John Updike. Copyright John Updike, 1963.
Jonathan Cape Ltd.: *The Old Man and the Sea* by Ernest Hemingway with acknowledgement to the Executors of the Ernest Hemingway Estate.
Ernest Hemingway, excerpted from *The Old Man and the Sea*. Copyright 1952 Ernest Hemingway; copyright renewed © 1980 Mary Hemingway. Reprinted with the permission of Charles Scribner's Sons.
Methuen & Co. Ltd.: *A Sea Burden* by C. Fox Smith.

(Acknowledgements continued on page 127)

Introduction

Boatopia was born when Françoise Legrand and I met one another. For years she had been taking photographs of boats, their masts, yards, rigging and other accoutrements. For years I had been reading and collecting stories and poems, passages and paragraphs about ships, the sea and rivers. Before long we decided to put our collections of pictures and words together.

From then on, we shared many voyages and found we had the same feeling, as land was left behind, of entering a new world, less encumbered, sometimes more dangerous, always more romantic and infinitely more unpredictable than the land-locked world of daily drudge.

We sailed in a run-down old caïque to the Pelagian Islands, about half-way between Sicily and Tunisia, went Greek-island-hopping in a yacht in the Aegean; and in Venice, haggled with a gondolier over the price of a wildly expensive half-hour glide along the Grand Canal.

Everywhere Françoise looked for the textures, shapes, forms and visual juxtapositions that are the essence of her photographic imagery. Art and boats are in her blood. Her great-grandfather, Antonio Fradeletto, founded the *Biennale*, the bi-annual art festival in Venice; her half-brother, Charles Ward, builds ships' lifeboats in Norfolk.

I started to study the sea and ships when I flew over the Atlantic and the North Sea with RAF Coastal Command. Later at Oxford, I read medieval texts on seafaring and navigation, Icelandic sagas, the records of master mariners such as Christopher Columbus, Vasco de Gama, Captain Cook and John Cabot. I searched for rare old sea shanties and historic logs, talked to boat builders, yacht designers and to any young or ancient mariner who could steer me towards something special they had read about ships and sailing.

Françoise and I explored shipping in great ports like Marseilles and in St Katharine's Docks by the Tower of London, went to sea with fishermen in remote islands off the coasts of Greece, Italy and in the Hebrides, were invited on board a millionaire's yacht, complete with 'floor-to-floor wheelhouse carpeting', and on to a fine old three-masted barquentine, with square-rigged fore-mast, fore-and-aft rigged main- and mizzen-masts.

Back in England, Françoise worked in her darkroom while I continued the search in libraries and maritime museums. We have picked the most evocative photographs and put them together with the most gripping and human stories about boats, the sea and rivers.

G.H.

The Way of a Ship

There be three things which are too wonderful for me,
Yea, four which I know not:
The way of an eagle in the air;
The way of a serpent upon a rock;
The way of a ship in the midst of the sea;
And the way of a man with a maid.

Old Testament, Proverbs: xxx

Yacht design as carried on at the present is rather like making love to a woman. The approach is completely empirical. At the end, the male, even though he might be successful, usually has no idea of just how and why he succeeded.

Professor E. J. Richards, at a conference on yacht design

Alan Hollingsworth brought these two quotations together in *The Way of a Yacht*.

* * *

Ships have temperaments. By some metamorphosis, the' coming together of timbers, iron, brass, rope, canvas and the rest throbs with life and individuality. And it even *sounds* like it! The creaks, slaps, groans, gurgles are lifelike responses to the stresses and strains of a ship's passage through water. Although a human's essential habitat is dry land, so much of the earth's surface is covered with water that it was natural right from the beginning that man would be driven by an inner urge, as well as through necessity, to build vessels that would carry him over the seas and along the rivers.

* * *

In the very beginning men went down, not to the sea but to quiet waters, and not in ships but in anything that would float: logs that could be straddled, rafts of wood or of bundles of reeds, perhaps even inflated skins.

But these were floats, not boats. The first true boat – something that would carry a man upon water and at the same time keep him dry – was very likely the dugout, although experiments with bound reeds or with skins stretched over light frames must have been made quite early too. And, when the desire or need arose for something bigger than what could be hollowed out of the largest logs available, the boat made of planks came into being. This was one of prehistoric man's most outstanding achievements; the credit for it probably goes to the Egyptians of the fourth millennium B.C.

As long as they stayed in shallow waters, men could propel their boats with punting poles. Farther out they used their hands – and this led them to devise the paddle, a wooden hand as it were, and soon afterward the oar. Then they hit upon something that revolutionized travel: they learned how to use the wind. For the first time they harnessed a force other than their own muscles, their servants', their animals' or their wives'. It was a discovery whose effects reached down the ages: from this moment on, the easiest and cheapest way of transporting bulky loads over distances of any appreciable length was by water. This is the point at which the story of the ancient mariners really starts; the scene again is Egypt, or perhaps Mesopotamia.

In southern Egypt archaeologists have found hundreds of pictures of boats which, shortly before 2900 B.C., were drawn helter-skelter on rock outcrops or which were included as part of the decoration on pottery. Among them are some which show, stepped amidships or forward of amidships, a mast with a broad squaresail hung upon it.

The Ancient Mariners, Lionel Casson

* * *

Men contrived to evolve the first arts of seamanship, the handling of their dangerous craft when wind brought waves, and when inshore currents swirled them from their course. They had to learn how to react to all the multitudinous effects of wind on the water through which they sought to drive their boats; and as today yachtsmen find fascination in the same study and practice, so, too, are they often mystified by the problems of wind and water which are at the root of seamanship. But in some respects it was the ancient and not the modern seamen who had crucial advantages.

Always to be remembered is the fact that what modern man has gained in philosophical ability has been won at the cost of atrophying some useful and once instinctive powers – accurate observation, memory that did not require records, sense of direction and locality that had no need of instruments or maps, smell (often so invaluable to the seaman), kinship with natural phenomena – all now mislaid in the Broadways of industrial civilization.

A philosopher once remarked that the human mind is a poor thing to use for reasoning about the nature of reality, since it originally evolved in order to help the swinging monkey find nuts. The first seamen had passed beyond the swinging for nuts. But, hunters and fishermen, they were harshly pressed to find the equivalent; and the equivalent too, of the monkey's fur and home up among the leaves, for the more complicated 'civilized' ways of keeping alive had not yet been revealed to them. The earlier instincts were intact. Early seamanship, and even much that was achieved during historical times, will never be understood unless this is remembered.

In our own day we have the examples of the unlettered men who, a generation ago, were often placed in charge of steam-trawlers that remained at sea for weeks on end, and yet they never thought to consult the charts provided by the owners which remained in their first folds year after year. These men when making a landfall in thick weather, could identify it though they may have faced it last a decade or more before. So, too, skippers of fishing-smacks found their way to a precise spot on the fishing-grounds and back to port again without chart or accurate compass.

Of such is the essence of ancient seafaring, beyond the comprehension of the sophisticated. Research in recent years has shown that birds conduct their migrations by means of celestial navigation, using the directions of the sun and stars for course, their altitude for position. There is evidence that fish do likewise, making the necessary allowance for the refraction of light. Man, driven by necessity, might distantly have approached these achievements.

The behaviour of the winds, the appearance of the clouds, of the sun at its rising and setting, of the moon and rainbows, the behaviour of the fish and birds, the feel of the air and the temperature, were the guides that long experience has been able to establish as indications of tomorrow's weather, on which life might depend.

A History of Seamanship, Douglas Phillips-Birt

* * *

Whether it's a longing for adventure, or an archetypal yearning to shuffle off earth-bound cares, or the romance, silence and mystery of the sea, something stirs within us the moment we cast off and move gently away from land. And there is almost nothing that people will not go to sea in. The sea is there and anything that is (or looks as if it is!) watertight is enough to tempt a man or a woman to set sail.

* * *

In the West Indies, one of the favourite diversions is watching the parade of yachts that stream into the islands from across the Atlantic. We don't have all the entertainment facilities like TV and the latest movies, but it is real fun and games to see what manages to get across the ocean from the other side.

In the years I have based in West Indian ports operating a charter yacht, I have seen innumerable voyagers reach the islands. The extremes have been extreme, from the ultimate in luxury such as the yacht *Half-0* . . . to the German who arrived in a folding kayak. It is said that anything watertight cast adrift off the coast of Portugal will eventually end up in the West Indies, such as the glass fishnet floats that drift in, and some of the vessels that arrive would seem to have less chance (and are much less watertight), and even less speed potential, than the glass floats. On them, the people who have made the passage offer many extremes, and the collection is one of the wackiest set of wayfarers that ever descended on an area. Not all of them are wacky, of course; many are sensible, forward-looking people who plan well and execute their voyages with fine seamanship, but one tends to remember the more oddball types. They make the best stories when Caribbean sailors gather in a cockpit for a session of yarning and reminiscing.

Half-0's was the ultimate in the sensible, well-planned voyages. She was a brand-new North Sea trawler type of hull with all the latest equipment. The owner wanted to cruise in comfort and safety with cost no particular object, and she had radar, loran, RDF, auto-pilot, ship-to-shore, roll dampers, and the whole list. Creature comforts were attended to by deep freeze, hot and cold water (tons of it), a galley that would make a hotel chef drool, and the supplies to go with it. I never saw a more comfortable, relaxed lot.

At the other end of the scale was the bearded German doctor who arrived in the kayak amid much fanfare and eventual publicity my first winter in St. Thomas, V.I. Now this was a truly amazing performance! He was some seventy-odd days at sea in the tropics yet was not badly

St Katharine's Dock by
the Tower of London.
The dead-eyes of the
main shrouds on the
Kathleen & May, a
wooden topsail trading
schooner which sailed in
British coastal waters.

sun-burned, nor did he have a very good crop of salt-water boils. He also had the world's best varnish and chrome. The varnished spars, paddles, and cockpit coaming were in good shape, and the chrome was unpitted.

The vast majority of arrivals fall between these extremes. For some, it is the result of a lifelong dream; to others it is just another pond to cross. There are a few who have lost track of the number of crossings they have made, so often have they done it.

Seawise, Donald M. Street, Jr.

* * *

The sails were spread out, wide and high – the two lower studding-sails stretching out on each side far beyond the deck; the topmost studding-sails spreading out fearlessly above them; still higher, the two royal studding-sails, looking like two kites flying from the same string, and the highest of all, the little sky-sail, the apex of the pyramid, seeming actually to touch the stars and to be out of reach of human hand.

One of the seamen wrote: 'I was so lost in the sight, I forgot the presence of the man who came out with me until he said (for he, too, rough old man-of-war's man as he was, had been gazing at the show) half to himself, still looking at the marble sails – "How quietly they do their work!"'

Two Years Before the Mast, Richard Henry Dana

* * *

There is no more thrilling sensation I know of than sailing. It comes as near to flying as man has got to yet – except in dreams. The wings of the rushing wind seem to be bearing you onward, you know not where. You are no longer the slow, plodding, puny thing of clay, creeping tortuously upon the ground; you are a part of Nature! Your heart is throbbing against hers. Her glorious arms are round you, raising you up against her heart! Your spirit is at one with hers; your limbs grow light! The voices of the air are singing to you. The earth seems far away and little; and the clouds so close above your head, are brothers, and you stretch your arms to them.

Three Men in a Boat, Jerome K. Jerome

* * *

But let it not be imagined that sailing is a sport only for the gifted few. I have remarked that it is the *matching* of measured skill with measured danger. That is the sweet thing about it. Provided the skill and the difficulty of the undertaking balance, their degree makes little odds: the pleasure will be as intense, and as honourable.

It is a sport which can be enjoyed from the very first day's bungling. I was a landlubber boy of eight when a derelict duck-punt washed up on the Essex mud-flats where I was spending the holidays. I stepped a willow-pole (of all timbers!) for mast, in a bit of old iron. A sack ripped open served for squaresail. It was a peculiar rig, with a string from each corner of the sail – two I controlled with my hands, two I trimmed with my bare toes, and I steered (perceptibly) with a board tucked under my arm. No *America Cup* contest certainly; but the rapture of spanking along before the wind at a round knot-and-a-half! Sliding over the mud in a few inches of water, and jeering at the proper yachts stuck fast till the next tide! Vermin that I was, I used to hail them and offer them a tow.

Other moments of intense excitement came later. Being taught in fog and a rising wind to handle a lugger, for example, by an old Downs pilot in carpet-slippers. Or later again, when I had signed as crew of a coaster: Captain and Mate went trustingly below for their dinner, I had never steered with a wheel before, and I took her on the spring flood through Bardseye Sound like a waltzing mouse. It made the gulls giddy to watch, but we hit nothing, and by the time the skipper came on deck again we were through, and I was holding the course like an old hand.

Sailing, Richard Hughes (*The Saturday Book*)

* * *

Building a boat is like giving birth except that a boat arrives in this world 'fully grown', with its character, personality and quirks of nature already developed. Fibreglass, as a functional material, has its place in boat-building but its inertness cannot match the warmth and living qualities of elm, mahogany, teak and oak.

* * *

During these years of war, port and sherry have been accumulating the other side of the Bay of Biscay, ready for us to purchase; and so it is with timber: all our best timbers – Canadian rock elm for bent timbers, Honduras mahogany for planking and joinery work, teak for deckhouses have been growing and I am certain have been cut and seasoned by the owners of the forest, ready for shipment when the time came. And these trees, not knowing there was a war on and that men over here were expected to work on so little food, will have grown calmly and naturally and as good as ever they grew; and at the moment we have timber as good as ever we had before, though we have not quite the selection of sizes in Honduras mahogany I should like. So I cannot see any timber troubles, except in our own home-grown oak, etc. (all that was seasoned was used during the war); but this will be put right in a short time.

Letter from Uffa Fox to Richard Hughes (*The Saturday Book*)

* * *

Arthur Ransome is known most of all for *Swallows and Amazons* which he wrote in 1930. But long before then, his life was varied and eventful. Throughout World War I, Ransome was a foreign correspondent in Russia where he fell in love with Trotsky's secretary, Eugenia Shelapina – and even defeated Lenin in a game of chess! A few years later, in 1921-22, *Racundra* was built, the boat he had been planning for years – 9 metres overall, 3½ metres in beam, heavily built with an oak centreboard and a 3½-ton iron keel, her cabin was the answer to Arthur Ransome's dream of 'a place where a man can live and work as comfortably and twice as pleasantly as in any room ashore'.

Houses are but badly built boats so firmly aground that you cannot think of moving them.

They are definitely inferior things, belonging to the vegetable not the animal world, rooted and stationary, incapable of gay transition. I admit, doubtfully, as exceptions, snail-shells and caravans. The desire to build a house is the tired wish of a man content thenceforward with a single anchorage. The desire to build a boat is the desire of youth, unwilling yet to accept the idea of a final resting-place.

It is for that reason, perhaps, that, when it comes, the desire to build a boat is one of those that cannot be resisted. It begins as a little cloud on a serene horizon. It ends by covering the whole sky, so that you can think of nothing else. You must build to regain your freedom. And always you comfort yourself with the thought that yours will be the perfect boat, the boat that you may search the harbours of the world for and not find.

That is the story of *Racundra*. Years of planning went into her before ever a line was drawn on paper. She was to be a cruising boat that one man could manage if need be, but on which three could live comfortably. She was to have writing-table and bookcase, a place for a typewriter, broad bunks where a man might lay him down and rest without bruising knee and elbow with each unconsidered movement. She was to carry her dinghy on deck to avoid that troublesome business of towing, which has brought so many good dinghies to their latter end. She should not be fast, but she should be fit to keep the sea when other little boats were scuttling for shelter. In fact, she was to be the boat that every man would wish who likes to move from port to port – a little ship in which, in temperate climates, a man might live from year's end to year's end.

'Racundra's' First Cruise, Arthur Ransome

* * *

Francis Chichester knew he would have to rest during the first solo sailing race across the Atlantic in 1960 and he sets out to study how a yacht could sail without a helmsman:

Every Sunday morning I took a bus to Kensington Gardens where I watched the model yachts being sailed across the Round Pond. I reckoned that if a model yacht can be sailed across the Round Pond without a helmsman, then my yacht could be sailed across the Atlantic in the same way. I bought an excellent book on model yacht sailing, and incidentally learned a lot about ocean racing from it though I dare say the author would be surprised to hear it. My new design was in principle a wind vane, which would always weathercock into wind. In fact it was a mast which could rotate in a socket at the stern of the yacht, with a flat sail instead of a metal vane. As soon as the yacht was sailing to my satisfaction I would lock the vane to the tiller. If the yacht came up into wind, the vane would be moved round with the yacht, and the wind would press on the side of it. This would pull on the tiller until the yacht had been steered back on to its original heading, when the vane would be weathercocked again, and do no work as long as the yacht kept on its original heading. The model yacht book told me that the area of the vane must be four and a half times that of the rudder, and so I designed my vane

Opposite page. The Nore Lightship. Lightships were anchored in dangerous waters to act as a lighthouse. The Nore is a sandbank in the Thames estuary lying off the approach to the river Medway.

sail to be 45 square feet. The chief problem in design was to make all the parts, the stays, and the spars, strong enough to stand up to a gale, or even a storm, without being so heavy that it would require too much wind to weathercock the vane. I cannot describe how ugly it looked on the beautiful *Gipsy Moth*.

The Lonely Sea and the Sky, Sir Francis Chichester

* * *

Racing was excellent but we were far from satisfied with the performance of the boat. The first three days we spent every evening arguing about the changes we could make to improve its performance. Morale got lower and lower. I was in despair. Then Owen Parker, who had first tuned the boat, reappeared on the scene to sail with us for the second half of the week. He listened to all our woes and heard the various proposals we were considering. The next morning he took a firm grip on the situation. As we went down to the starting line he said very forcibly in the hearing of the whole crew, 'Look, sir, you've got this bloody boat. Stop arguing about it and sail the bloody boat you've got. Then we might begin to get somewhere!' This put an end to all the arguments. Morale rose again. We came second in that race and on the last day, although he had then left us, we won. It was due to the impact of a remarkable personality. There always comes a point when you have to stop arguing about the boat and concentrate on sailing what you have got.

Sailing – A Course of My Life, Edward Heath

* * *

Like men and women, ships can die a natural death through old age or they can come to a violent end. The Goodwin Sands, at the entrance to the Straits of Dover from the North Sea, are known as 'the graveyard of ships'. Thomas Treanor, a seamen's chaplain at the end of the 19th century, has left us this eyewitness account of what the Goodwins can do to a ship.

As to the depth of the great sandbank, borings have been made down to the chalk to a depth of seventy-eight feet – a fact which might have been fairly conjectured from the depth of water inside the Goodwins, down to the chalky bottom being nine or ten fathoms, while the depth close outside the Goodwins, where the outer edge of the sands is sheer and steep, is fifteen fathoms, deepening a mile and a half further off the Goodwins to twenty-eight fathoms.

The ships wrecked on the Goodwins go down into it very slowly, but they sometimes literally fall off the steep outer edge into the deep water above described.

One still bright autumn morning I witnessed a tragedy of that description. On the forenoon of November 30, 1888, I was on the deck of a barque, the Maritzburg, bound to Port Natal. I had visited the men in the forecastle, and indeed all hands fore and aft, as *Missions to Seamen* chaplain; and to them all I spoke, and was, in fact, speaking of that only 'Name under heaven whereby we must be saved,' when my eyes were riveted, as I gazed right under the sun, by the drama being enacted away to the southward.

There I saw, three miles off, our two lifeboats of Kingsdown and Walmer, each in tow of a steamer which came to their aid, making for the Goodwins, and on the outer edge of the

Goodwins I beheld a hapless brig, with sails set, aground. I saw her at that distance lifted by the heavy sea, and at that distance I saw the great tumble of the billows. That she had heavily struck the bottom I also saw, for crash! – and even at that distance I verily seemed to hear the crash – away went her mainmast over her side, and the next instant she was gone, and had absolutely and entirely disappeared. I could not believe my eyes, and rubbed them and gazed again and yet again.

She had perished with all hands. The lifeboats, fast as they went, were just too late, and found nothing but a nameless boat, bottom upwards, and a lifebelt, and no one ever knew her nationality or name. She had struck the Goodwins, and had been probably burst open by the shock, and then, dragged by the great offtide to the east, had rolled into the deep water outside the Goodwins and close to its dreadful edge.

Heroes of the Goodwin Sands, Thomas Stanley Treanor

* * *

Cape of Good Hope
Tuesday, 23 February 1830
Much as I have heard of shipwrecks, yet I am convinced that no one who has not experienced it can form any adequate idea of all the horrors of it.

We had been going on prosperously until the evening of Saturday, the 13th. We had been for some days annoyed by contrary winds which prevented our reaching the Cape. On the day in question, an observation was taken in the middle of the day and we were then far from land, but the wind and the violent current, carried us with such rapidity, added to the darkness of the night, that at 10 o'clock, there was a cry of 'breakers ahead' – immediately the helm was put down and every effort made to back the ship, but alas it was too late, and in two minutes we struck.

I had been in bed for half an hour, and with the exception of one lady, were the only ones of the party who had unfortunately taken off our clothes. A few seconds sufficed to assemble all the party on deck, where nothing can equal the scene which took place, the married ladies all clinging to their husbands.

We all assembled together, not venturing to go forward to speak to anyone occupied with the ship. The masts were cut down, but the repeated and severe shocks of the ship were such as to make us all tumble about, nor was there anything secure by which we could hold. A small boat was lowered, and the second officer sent in it to see whether there was a possibility of getting on shore anywhere. We were to remain in the ship to the last moment, deeming it safer than risking our lives in the boat, surrounded as we appeared to be on all sides by breakers, but before any tidings arrived of the boat, the shocks of the ship became so frightful that we literally stood on the deck expecting every moment she would shiver to pieces.

She was filling fast with water and it was then declared that our last hope rested on getting into the longboat and keeping out at sea until the moon should give sufficient light for us to ascertain nearly where we were.

The bulwarks were cut down, and the boat launched into the water upon which there was a cheering hurrah from all the men at its being safe in the water but this was followed by a moment of awful silence and intense agony when one voice was heard to ejaculate 'Our last hope is gone, the boat has gone off, and is upon the breakers'. At the same moment one of the sailors dashed into the water and caught the rope just in time to save it, it was brought round to the stern, and we were all taken out at the gangway, carried along the side of the ship, and then with a rope secured and lowered down one by one into the boat.

We were fourteen females, three gentlemen accompanied us, being all it could contain with any degree of safety. By this time the small boat hailed us, they had found a landing place on a desert island, took us in tow and conveyed us to it.

Women Under Sail, Basil Greenhill and Ann Giffard

Mary Saunders, who wrote the above letter, had sailed from Portsmouth on the 14th October 1829 for Madras, on the *Lady Holland*, a full-rigged merchant ship of 405 tons. All the passengers and crew were saved and eventually rescued from Dassen Island, forty miles north of Cape Town.

* * *

I was on the bridge when the torpedo struck. It was the loudest sound I had ever heard. The great column of water threw the matchwood of the outswung starboard boats high into the air and the fall of debris seemed interminable. The ship lurched heavily to port. This – my mind recorded with strange clarity – was what the text books called 'the initial heel', and by the time I had reached the port lifeboats the ship was almost on an even keel again.

The men worked quietly with many white faces but no panic and the two remaining boats were freed and lowered. A hurried census showed many missing: two officers, three engineers, two radio-men, the entire watch in the engine-room, six gunners – nineteen men in all.

I made a quick decision, and was gratified to realise that I felt no pang of fear at this stage.

'I am going back,' I said to the Chief Engineer. 'Take over my boat for a while: lie off and wait for me'.

'You must be quick, Mister,' the Captain called from the other boat. 'She is going fast'.

'Let me come with you, sir!' It was the senior cadet in the Captain's boat. Two days ago he had had his seventeenth birthday. I looked at the Captain and, after a moment's pause, the Old Man nodded his head.

The boy climbed nimbly on board. The ship was, as the Captain said, sinking fast, her stern almost awash. I made for the engine-room and directed the boy to the wrecked cabins along the starboard side. The silence was sepulchral, accentuated rather than disturbed by a sound like water rushing over a weir. It was the sea pouring into the dying ship.

The dark and tangled chaos of the engine-room, thick with the sour stench of the explosive, was obviously nothing but a tomb and the one figure I found was mutilated beyond my aid. I came out to the daylight with a sense of immense relief and met the boy who said no word but simply shook his head. He looked white and sick.

Opposite page. Heraklion. On the north coast of Crete, largest and most southerly of the Greek islands, the port was founded in the 9th century by the Saracens near Knossos, capital of the Minoan Kingdom.

The ship's stern was now completely submerged, and we could feel the deck falling away beneath us. We slipped into the sea and swam away. We had not gone far when a rumbling crescendo of sound drew our eyes back to the ship. It was a wonderful and terrible sight. About a hundred feet of her bow pointed straight out of the sea, trembling under the stress of a thunderous noise, as the great engines, the anchors and cables tore their way through the bowels of the ship – a dreadful sound that scribed ineffaceably deep into the tablet of my memory. Then the bow slid quickly under in a boiling of white foam and flotsam.

The Seaman's World, Stanley Simpson (selected by Ronald Hope)

* * *

Coming to terms with a ship and with its crew is as complex, strange, personal and unpredictable as any human relationship. Captain James Cook, one of the greatest of all navigators, had sailed further and for longer than any mariner before him, more than 160,000 miles across the seas, adding a quarter to what was known of the world at the time. In the 1770s, while on board His Majesty's Sloop *Resolution*, at anchor for six months in the Friendly Islands (now known as the Tonga Islands), he reflects while awaiting a propitious time to carry out the Admiralty's instructions to search for the North West Passage:

First as regards the People under my command. Such a long period of relative inactivity must always put a strain upon the Discipline of the Ships. I do know that they look upon me as a man of undoubted severity and this I have never discouraged. Indeed, it is something I have at all times fostered, both in my manner and bearing, my officers all being much younger men and only myself by practice and experience able to enforce Discipline by a glance. I am seldom able to relax, nor have been these many years, so that when I see myself in the mirror I am forced to the realization that by habit my features have become set into an expression that is something severe. Capt. Clerke manages to temper this with his humour, but I lack this advantage, and if I be not much liked by some it does ensure that I am always obeyed and so absolute master in my own house, though living in close company with others long years at a stretch. Nevertheless the strain of it is at times almost beyond bearing and when I see the flaunting, libidinous behaviour of some of the women of these islands, they so handsome and free with their favours, I confess there are moments when I would be happy to exchange the isolation of command for the carefree abandon of a Midshipman's life.

The Last Voyage, Hammond Innes

* * *

Seafaring has always been more than a job: it is a calling and the call often comes early in a man's life. Son of the master of a coastal vessel, William Slade leaves school at the age of twelve to become ship's boy in the last years of the small wooden merchant sailing ships:

Opposite page. Plymouth. At the western approach to the English Channel, point of departure for Sir Francis Drake, Sir Walter Raleigh – and Sir Francis Chichester. From Plymouth in 1620 the Pilgrim Fathers set sail in the Mayflower.

Cromer. Weathered hull of an old fishing boat anchored near the jetty of a cliff-side market town on the north Norfolk coast.

Life in those early days was certainly no bed of roses. When at sea I was often miserably seasick and as Father never felt seasick in his life he had no sympathy for me and perhaps it was just as well. When we got in harbour, the cargo had to be winched out and I had to do my full share. In addition, when the others had their rest between meals, there was always something for me to do. The daily routine was: get up 6 a.m., light the fire and get breakfast going, then on the winch. If there was a minute to spare, run into the galley, see to the fire, etc.; 8 a.m. take the breakfast down for the crew. After breakfast the others had a rest, but not the boy: he washed up dishes and cleared away the mess, hurriedly got the dinner going and then the shouting commenced. 'Come on, slowcoach, it's time to start work. They are waiting for you.' At dinner time the same thing again. After tea the crew had their freedom, but the boy still had a lot to do. The stove had to be cleaned out, the fire laid in ready for the morning and the potatoes had to be peeled for dinner the next day. It was always 9 p.m. before the boy finished work and after a wash it was time to go to bed. How I longed to be promoted to ordinary seaman!

Out of Appledore, W. J. Slade

* * *

September 19, 1900. Indentures are drawn up for Vincent Large, aged fifteen, to join the *Shakespeare* as an apprentice. His widowed mother had paid the owners a premium of £20 (the equivalent, perhaps, of £2,000 or $2,500 now) which entitled him to work for four years — without pay. Captain Large, as he became, recalls his first two days at sea, two days of seasickness and lack of sleep:

I presented myself to Captain Richardson and said, 'Sir, I have changed my mind about going to sea. Could you please put into port and land me?'

He regarded me with astonishment, his mouth half open as if he was about to explode with anger. Then observing my earnest expression his face relaxed and he smiled as he replied, 'My boy, I can't, and even if I could I wouldn't. You've made your bed and now you'll have to lie on it. Stick to it and you will find it is not too bad.'

Realising that I had made a fool of myself, I muttered a few apologetic words and turned away feeling completely humiliated. That night when I turned in, the weather was good and the ship was riding evenly on a rather heavy swell. I was so tired that I slept soundly, and when I woke next morning I felt like a different person. Getting out of my bunk, I went on deck where I found that although it was cold, the weather was bright and sunny and the decks were drying off rapidly.

I sat down on the main hatch, and for the first time since the beginning of the storm I looked about me and took in my surroundings. After a while I began to think that life wasn't so bad, after all, and being at sea was not so hard. I watched the masts moving lazily against the sky and listened to the creaking of the yards and the whipping of the sails. I watched the white canvas bellying in the light breeze, and stared in fascination at the long ocean swells as they gently but remorselessly rolled past us. I watched the sailors moving about the decks, the helmsman at the wheel and the mate keeping watch. Suddenly I felt glad that I was one of

Limassol. The main port on Cyprus, stepping-stone between the continents of Europe, Asia and Africa.

them, vaguely realising that I had met and overcome a crisis in my life. And I was ravenously hungry!

After walking round the deck for a time I went to the galley and asked for some food. The cook gave me something, but not nearly enough, so later in the day I decided the time had arrived to broach the case of provisions which my mother had so thoughtfully packed for me.

I had already learned the unwritten law of the half-deck that all comforts had to be pooled. No apprentice dared to put any food aside for himself or to lock his sea chest, because that was a sign of lack of trust and faith in his fellows. If a sea chest was ever locked it would soon be forced open; if left unlocked, it was never molested. For some unknown reason I decided that tomatoes had more appeal than anything else, so I took a few tins from the chest. I gave some to the other apprentices and then went to work on my own share. Not having eaten for over two days, I made a veritable feast of those tomatoes. Sad to relate, my gluttony had the inevitable result, and within half an hour I was violently ill once again. This time it was not because of the sea and I recovered quickly, but it was a long while before I was able to face a tinned tomato again.

Windjammer 'Prentice, Vincent Large

* * *

There was no sleep on board that night. Most seamen remembered in their life one or two such nights of a culminating gale. Nothing seems left of the whole universe but darkness, clamour, fury – and the ship. And like the last vestige of a shattered creation she drifts, bearing an anguished remnant of sinful mankind, through the distress, tumult, and pain of an avenging terror. No one slept in the forecastle. The tin oil-lamp suspended on a long string, smoking, described wide circles; wet clothing made dark heaps on the glistening floor; a thin layer of water rushed to and fro. In the bed-places men lay booted, resting on elbows and with open eyes. Hung-up suits of oil-skin swung out and in, lively and disquieting like reckless ghosts of decapitated seamen dancing in a tempest. No one spoke and all listened.

Outside the night moaned and sobbed to the accompaniment of a continuous loud tremor as of innumerable drums beating far off. Shrieks passed through the air. Tremendous dull blows made the ship tremble while she rolled under the weight of the seas toppling on her deck. At times she soared up swiftly as if to leave this earth for ever, then during interminable moments fell through a void with all the hearts on board of her standing still, till a frightful shock, expected and sudden, started them off again with a big thump.

The Nigger of the 'Narcissus', Joseph Conrad

* * *

4 December 1831

I am writing this for the first time on board. It is now about 1 o'clock, and I intend sleeping in my hammock, I did so last night and experienced a most ludicrous difficulty in getting into it; my great fault of jockeyship was in trying to put my legs in first. The hammock being suspended, I thus only succeeded in pushing it away without making any progress in inserting my own body. The correct method is to sit accurately in centre of bed, then give yourself a dexterous twist, and your head and feet come into their respective places. After a little time I daresay I shall, like others, find it very comfortable.

The Voyage of the Beagle, Charles Darwin

* * *

No man will be a sailor who has contrivance enough to get himself into a jail; for being in a ship is being in a jail, with the chance of being drowned . . . A man in a jail has more room, better food, and commonly better company.

The Life of Samuel Johnson, James Boswell

* * *

A sea trip does you good when you are going to have a couple of months of it, but, for a week, it is wicked.

You start on Monday with the idea implanted in your bosom that you are going to enjoy yourself. You wave an airy adieu to the boys on shore, light your biggest pipe, and swagger about the deck as if you were Captain Cook, Sir Francis Drake, and Christopher Columbus all rolled into one. On Tuesday, you wish you hadn't come. On Wednesday, Thursday, and Friday, you wish you were dead. On Saturday you are able to swallow a little beef tea, and to sit up on deck, and answer with a wan, sweet smile when kind-hearted people ask you how you feel now. On Sunday, you begin to walk about again, and take solid food. And on Monday morning, as, with your bag and umbrella in your hand, you stand by the gunwale, waiting to step ashore, you begin to thoroughly like it.

Three Men in a Boat, Jerome K. Jerome

* * *

Beards and moustaches may be grown by permission of the Captain. When permission is granted a full set must be grown (i.e. a moustache or a beard by itself is not allowed) and shaving must be discontinued, the hairs being trimmed with scissors only to achieve neatness and uniformity. 'Comic Opera' facial adornments are forbidden. Hair must be kept short and the forelock should not reach below the eyebrows.

The Naval Ratings Handbook, 1938 (British Admiralty)

* * *

At five feet two inches, Clare Francis is the smallest person to have sailed the Atlantic alone. She took part in the *Observer Single-Handed Transatlantic Race* and completed the course in 29 days. Most *men* care little enough about what they look like under rough conditions at sea. As an attractive woman, Clare Francis gives us this moving and human account of how she tried to remain fresh and feminine, and ends with a rueful comment on 'the way of the ship':

When I was halfway through my long breakfast I suddenly decided to brave the cold and have a wash because I knew I wouldn't have the courage to face another for a long time. I had been inspired by one item of the contents of the parcel my godmother had given me. It was some

Yves St Laurent talcum powder and, when I sniffed it, it smelt so good that I longed to smell like that too. It was not that I smelled badly – although I could not be put to the acid test of having people sit beside me, distend their nostrils and faint or otherwise – but I was musty and salty, rather like an ancient sea relic. I longed to feel fresh and vaguely feminine again, although I wondered if I'd still recognise the feeling.

As I washed and powdered myself I was amazed to discover that I had a new body. There were bones and hollows where none had been before. I had always thought my hips were naturally wide, but they were really quite narrow. If I could manage to stay that way my clothes would look marvellous. But, with a sigh, I had to admit that a bikini would not look as good because, along with my hips, my bosom had almost entirely disappeared. I hadn't been much of a Jayne Mansfield to start with but I was still a bit put out. It was the principle of the thing.

With so many sharp bones protruding, I was covered in a multitude of bruises which ranged through every colour from dirty orange to bright purple. On favourite spots like my knees and thighs they were arranged in clusters like exhibits at the Chelsea Flower Show. I was well practised in moving around the boat carefully, but when every single object was sharp, jutting or just plain hard, it was impossible to escape them all the time. The worst were the cleats. If they didn't get me on the ankle when I walked by, then they'd bang me on the knee as I crawled past. But it was my shins that had the most painful encounters and always with the sill of the main hatchway, which was both hard and sharp. In bad weather it was impossible not to receive bruises everywhere, for the motion of the boat was too wild to anticipate with any accuracy. It was a matter of clinging on and dodging the bits of boat as they came at you.

Come Hell or High Water, Clare Francis

Opposite page. St Tropez. Rich and successful artists and filmstars line up their yachts along the quay of this legendary port on the Côte d'Azur in the south of France.

The Lonely Sea and the Sky

The poet John Masefield ran away to sea early in his life, so he knew the sea at first hand, which is why Francis Chichester considered him the greatest of sea poets. Sir Francis said of Masefield's poem, *Sea Fever*: it 'gives in only twelve lines the key to my lifetime search for romance and adventure':

> I must down to the seas again, to the lonely sea and the sky,
> And all I ask is a tall ship and a star to steer her by,
> And the wheel's kick and the wind's song and the white sail's shaking,
> and a gray mist on the sea's face and a gray dawn breaking.
>
> I must down to the seas again, for the call of the running tide
> Is a wild call and a clear call that may not be denied;
> And all I ask is a windy day with the white clouds flying,
> And the flung spray and the blown spume, and the sea gulls crying.
>
> I must down to the seas again, to the vagrant gypsy life,
> To the gull's way and the whale's way where the wind's like a whetted knife;
> And all I ask is a merry yarn from a laughing fellow-rover,
> And quiet sleep and a sweet dream when the long trick's over.
>
> *Sea Fever*, John Masefield

* * *

A long solo voyage is a lonely journey. But *before* you embark it is a highly sociable affair, as friends and relatives gather round with presents, advice and good wishes, especially if you are a young woman 'going it alone' across the Atlantic.

'Now,' said Mother, 'are you taking enough food? Well, however much you think you have, I've just brought along a few extras.' Whereupon she went off in the direction of the car park, and disappeared.

'Where's Mother?' I asked a few minutes later. Jacques looked up and, turning pale, pointed behind me. An enormous cardboard box was making its way ponderously along the pontoon and under it were Mother's legs looking uncertain around the knees. Jacques leapt to the rescue and we were soon unloading tins of artichokes, asparagus, chestnuts, rich soups and other delicacies. 'Just a few essentials', said Mother. 'Now, have you got enough warm clothes?' Ever since my sister and I had left home Mother had been convinced that, if we weren't underfed, we were underclothed. Having once read an advertisement about some thermal underwear 'that generates its own heat' and an article about the wonders of nuclear energy on the same day, she was a great believer in thermo-nuclear underwear. Indeed, in the winter resort where my parents went ski-ing every year, she was famous for her thermo-nuclear knickers which, she swore, defied any number of sudden sittings in the snow.

Having given me a full set of her special underwear, Mother triumphantly held up a string of paper knickers. 'Much more practical,' she declared. 'Although I've brought a small bag of detergent and some clothes pegs as well, just in case you have the time.'

Come Hell or High Water, Clare Francis

* * *

I asked Francis Chichester about loneliness, just after he had returned from his second single-handed sail across the Atlantic. I had just returned from a long sojourn on a remote island, a day's sail off the south coast of Sicily. We compared our different experiences of isolation and of doing things alone.

The drawbacks of racing alone across the Atlantic may be obvious, but what are the advantages, which must be great to make one wish to do it again? *Loneliness*, which you would think a disadvantage, only lasts for a short period of time, while breaking contact with the land, and for a few hours after that. From then on it seems to me one is only in a long race. I mean, that if you were in a cross-country race you wouldn't worry about being alone, and a trip across the Atlantic is only a longer race. There is the obvious thrill of surging through the Atlantic swell and seas with all sail set, and lovely bow waves combing each side. There is the adventure of 3,000 miles of the Atlantic ahead of you. A voyage is like a classical drama: it starts slowly and works up with many adventurous incidents to the finish.

When I am alone on an adventure I become more efficient. I seem to be twice as efficient, and I become vitalized. I don't know why – perhaps it is because when I am with someone else I am concerned with their comfort or safety rather than getting on with the job. I have always been keen on doing things alone.

Atlantic Adventure, Sir Francis Chichester

* * *

63rd day

Can't believe it, but there it is: wind from the northwest, Force 5-6. How the hell is one supposed to go on like this? What have I done to you, Venus, and all the gods alike, to deserve this? And *Independent Television News* had the unbelievable cheek to ask, this morning, what do I do with my spare time! Spare time? By jove don't they realize what it is like out here? I row ten hours, almost every day. When I don't it's because, like today, I'm too damn tired to grasp an oar, let alone pull it and move a ton of boat against the wind. I am navigator, cook, deckhand, engine, photographer, radioman: you name, I've got to do it – who else? A storm could hit us without warning, so *Britannia* must be kept shipshape at all times. A day has twenty-four hours. I get up at 0500 GMT (0300 zone time); by 1200 GMT I have rowed five hours; a break until 1700 GMT and then row another five hours, till 2400 GMT – when I go, drop rather, to sleep till 0500 GMT and start again. Thus I sleep five hours in a row. I wake up every hour or two, but never mind. If I can, I catch another hour of sleep after midday. This leaves about eight hours when, in theory, I could do other things. In practice, I cannot row without resting in between, and this takes care of another two to three hours, during which I am too busy, just lying down to get my breath back, to do anything. And then I have to do everything else, as mentioned. Spare time? If I catch a dolphin every now and then, it's not for sport but because I need it, and it is bloody – literally – work, as dolphins are big and strong and jolly good fighters. It takes me an hour to clean up from beginning to end. No matter what one does, everything takes three to four times as long as it should on *Britannia* because she is so cramped, wet, rolling without pause, slippery . . . Spare time? If I can squeeze out any, I'd kill a shark if there are any around – hate the bastards! Might end up inside one of them in the near future, and I want to make sure that if that happens, I have good company. Rowed eight hours; steered west; could not cope against the wind any longer. Fagged out.

Britannia: Rowing Alone Across the Atlantic, John Fairfax

* * *

The best blood-sports are those where the only life in jeopardy is the sportsman's. Rock-climbing is one of these – but perhaps too lethal an example, since real addicts do not commonly live beyond middle-age. Single-handed cruising is another.

There is, of course, nothing foolhardy about such sports: that would be uninteresting except to boys. Rather it is a match between measured skill and measured danger. If at times the achievement seems foolhardy, that is because the adept can bank on a skill beyond common understanding and almost beyond belief. For skill of the first order does not come only from practice and study: it is inborn. Physical genius is as wide of average ability as mental genius is; and indeed if the hand on the paint-brush or the piano-keys can be inspired, why not the hand on the tiller? If Voss (who also sailed round the world in a dug-out canoe) could survive in a tiny pleasure-yacht through the heart of a great cyclone the mere fringe of which wrecked Yokohama: if Fred Rebell, with no previous experience of boat-sailing, could take an 18 ft. boat alone the 9,000 miles from Sydney to Los Angeles: if Uffa Fox could sail a racing canoe (a craft you or I would capsize in a swimming-bath) from Cowes to Brittany – well, Yehudi Menuhin can do some astounding things with his hands too, and so could Cézanne.

Slocum was the father of the sport, and it was born in a New England apple-orchard. Slocum was an elderly Yankee sea-captain without a ship when, towards the turn of the last century, an acquaintance offered him a new command. The offer was a wry joke; for the little *Spray* was hauled up rotting among the trees, riper than the windfalls round her. But Slocum had accepted the command and refused to see any joke in it – thereby turning it on the joker.

He rebuilt *Spray* from stem to stern with his own hands, launched her, embarked alone, and set her on an easterly course. The Banks fishermen were left behind. Encouraged by a vision (visions are not uncommon among single-handed seamen), he made Gibraltar. There he was warned not to enter the Mediterranean because of Barbary pirates – still active even then, in a diminished way. So Slocum turned about, and sailed for the Straits of Magellan. Here, too,

Opposite page. Sound of Raasay. The Sound separates remote lonely Raasay Island, narrow and some twelve miles long, from the Isle of Skye to the west, the largest island of the Inner Hebrides.

his dangers came in part from Man: the wild Fuegians. But Slocum sprinkled his deck with carpet-tacks, and so slept easy, having made each barefoot savage his own burglar-alarm. After appalling battles with contrary winds he at last burst out into the Pacific, and by way of Australia and Africa arrived home again — the first man in the history of Man to circumnavigate the globe alone.

Voss is the second great name (he did not sail single-handed, but none of his successive 'crews' lasted very long). Voss set out to prove a theory: that with a drogue or sea-anchor to regulate its drift a small craft — *any* small craft — can swim the most angry and mountainous seas. Accordingly Voss bought a fifty-year-old dug-out canoe from a Vancouver Island Indian (the skull of the builder was thrown in for good measure), decked her over, and stepped a row of stubby masts. He too circumnavigated the globe; and the only substantial damage *Tilikum* sustained was in an accident on dry land. Thus the doctrine of the sea-anchor was so firmly established that only in very recent years have the pundits begun to question it.

Yet genius itself is not infallible, and at sea that may be a final matter. No one knows how Voss died, in the end. No one knows for certain, either, just how Captain Slocum drowned.

Sailing, Richard Hughes (*The Saturday Book*)

About midnight the fog shut down again denser than ever before. One could almost 'stand on it'. It continued so for a number of days, the wind increasing to a gale. The waves rose high, but I had a good ship. Still, in the dismal fog I felt myself drifting into loneliness, an insect on a straw in the midst of the elements. I lashed the helm, and my vessel held her course, and while she sailed I slept.

During these days a feeling of awe crept over me. My memory worked with startling power. The ominous, the insignificant, the great, the small, the wonderful, the commonplace — all appeared before my mental vision in magical succession. Pages of my history were recalled which had been so long forgotten that they seemed to belong to a previous existence. I heard all the voices of the past laughing, crying, telling what I had heard them tell in many corners of the earth.

The loneliness of my state wore off when the gale was high and I found much work to do. When fine weather returned, then came the sense of solitude, which I could not shake off. I used my voice often, at first giving some order about the affairs of a ship, for I had been told that from disuse I should lose my speech. At the meridian altitude of the sun I called aloud, 'Eight bells', after the custom on a ship at sea. Again from my cabin I cried to an imaginary man at the helm, 'How does she head there?' and again, 'Is she on her course?' But getting no reply, I was reminded the more palpably of my condition. My voice sounded hollow on the empty air, and I dropped the practice. However, it was not long before the thought came to me that when I was a lad I used to sing; why not try that now, where it would disturb no one? My musical talent had never bred envy in others, but out on the Atlantic, to realize what it meant, you should have heard me sing. You should have seen the porpoises leap when I pitched my voice for the waves and the sea and all that was in it. Old turtles, with large eyes, poked their heads up out of the sea as I sang *Johnny Boker*, and *We'll Pay Darby Doyl for his*

Boots, and the like. But the porpoises were, on the whole, vastly more appreciative than the turtles; they jumped a deal higher. One day when I was humming a favourite chant, I think it was *Babylon's a-Falling*, a porpoise jumped higher than the bowsprit. Had the *Spray* been going a little faster she would have scooped him in.

Sailing Alone Around the World, Joshua Slocum

* * *

Confronting a storm at sea is like fighting God. All the powers in the universe seem to be against you and, in an extraordinary way, your irrelevance is at the same time both humbling and exalting.

Even as late as 1938 there were still thirteen ships, propelled by sail alone, engaged in carrying grain from south Australia to Europe – by way of Cape Horn, one of the most demanding tests of endurance and seamanship. Eric Newby sailed in 1939 with the *Moshulu*, a steel four-masted barque of 5,300 tons:

Moshulu continued to carry her sail and the storm entered its last and most impressive phase. We were cold and wet and yet too excited to sleep. Some stood on the fo'c'sle head but only for a short time as the force of the wind made it difficult to remain on two feet. Others stood beneath it and gazed out along the ship, watching the seas rearing up astern as high as a three-storeyed house. It was not only their height that was impressive but their length. Between the greatest of them there was a distance that could only be estimated in relation to the ship, as much as four times her entire length, or nearly a quarter of a mile. The seas approached very deliberately, black and shiny as jet, with smoking white crests gleaming in the sunshine, hissing as they came, hurling a fine spume into the air as high as the main yard.

I went aloft in the fore rigging, out of the comparative shelter of the foresail, into the top, and higher again to the cross-trees, where I braced myself to the backstays. At this height, 130 feet up, in a wind blowing 70 miles an hour, the noise was an unearthly scream. Above me was the naked topgallant yard and above that again the royal to which I presently climbed. I was now used to heights but the bare yard, gleaming yellow in the sunshine, was groaning and creaking on its tracks. The high whistle of the wind through the halliards sheaf, and above all the pale blue illimitable sky, cold and serene, made me deeply afraid and conscious of my insignificance.

Far below, the ship was an impressive sight. For a time the whole of the after deck would disappear, hatches, winches, everything, as the solid water hit it, and then, like an animal pulled down by hounds, she would rise and shake them from her, would come lifting out of the sea with her freeing ports spouting.

The Last Grain Race, Eric Newby

* * *

I need not tell you what it is to be knocking about in an open boat. I remember nights and days of calm, when we pulled, we pulled, and the boat seemed to stand still, as if bewitched within the circle of the sea horizon. I remember the heat, the deluge of rain-squalls that kept

us baling for dear life (but filled our water-cask), and I remember sixteen hours on end with a mouth dry as a cinder and a steering-oar over the stern to keep my first command head on to a breaking sea. I did not know how good a man I was till then. I remember the drawn faces, the dejected figures of my two men, and I remember my youth and the feeling that will never come back any more — the feeling that I could last for ever, outlast the sea, the earth, and all men; the deceitful feeling that lures us on to joys, to perils, to love, to vain effort — to death; the triumphant conviction of strength, the heat of life in the handful of dust, the glow in the heart that with every year grows dim, grows cold, grows small, and expires — and expires, too soon, too soon — before life itself.

Youth, Joseph Conrad

* * *

Three poets write about the wind and the sea: the successful American novelist John Updike is contemptuous and scathing, an unknown Welsh poet is awed and respectful, and for a fisherman, it is all in a day's work:

> Many-maned scud-thumper, tub
> of many whales, maker of worn wood, shrub-
> ruster, sky-mocker, rave!
> portly pusher of waves, wind-slave.

Winter Ocean, John Updike

* * *

> Great God! when he cometh,
> How the sea foameth
> At the breath of his nostrils,
>   The Blast of his mouth!
>   As it smites from the south —
> Foameth and spumeth
>   And roars on the shores!

A Song to the Wind from *Welsh Poetry Old and New* (translated by A.P. Graves)

* * *

> When the wind is in the East
> 'Tis neither good for man nor beast.
>
> When the wind is in the North
> The skilful fisher goes not forth.

Opposite page. Raasay Island. The old pier where steamers and ferries call from Skye, across the Sound of Raasay, the island to which Prince Charles Edward escaped after the up-rising of 1745.

When the wind is in the South
It blows the bait in the fish's mouth.

When the wind is in the West
Then it is at its very best.

Fisherman's Lore (Anonymous)

* * *

Anyone who has read Ernest Hemingway's *The Old Man and the Sea* remembers it. It is the most powerful story of deep-sea fishing ever written. The old man had not had a catch for eighty-four days. Then alone in the Gulf of Mexico, out of sight of land, 'he was fast to the biggest fish he had ever seen and bigger than he had ever heard of', a fish two feet longer than his own fishing skiff.

For three days of remorseless endurance, without a moment of respite, the great fish stayed at the end of the steel line, before the old man could harpoon it:

He took all his pain and what was left of his strength and his long gone pride and he put it against the fish's agony and the fish came over on to his side and swam gently on his side, his bill almost touching the planking of the skiff, and started to pass the boat, long, deep, wide, silver and barred with purple and interminable in the water.

The old man dropped the line and put his foot on it and lifted the harpoon as high as he could and drove it down with all his strength, and more strength he had just summoned, into the fish's side just behind the great chest fin that rose high in the air to the altitude of the man's chest. He felt the iron go in and he leaned on it and drove it further and then pushed all his weight after it.

Then the fish came alive, with his death in him, and rose high out of the water showing all his great length and width and all his power and his beauty. He seemed to hang in the air above the old man in the skiff. Then he fell into the water with a crash that sent spray over the old man and over all of the skiff.

The Old Man and the Sea, Ernest Hemingway

* * *

Some would say it is a simple life – away from it all. It can be, if you ignore the radio on board – and we don't carry a cassette player. It is certainly varied, at times physically exacting and mentally demanding, at others frustrating to the point of extreme boredom. There is an element of danger inseparable from the sport, whether from overstrained equipment on board or from other ships, especially when crossing traffic lanes in fog. The perils of the sea also help to bind a crew together, for every member of it knows that his life, like theirs, depends on their joint efforts. Is there ever fear at sea? Yes, of course. No one who has taken part in ocean racing would want to deny that; but action is often an effective antidote to fear and the need for action is seldom lacking in bad conditions at sea. And sometimes there is personal grief at the loss of a fellow sailor and, very rarely, at the loss of a boat. The sea always demands respect

Delos. The tiny island in the Greek Cyclades, where the sacred sanctuary of Apollo looks out to sea.

Scylla. In southern Italy, at the narrow entrance to the Straits of Messina, with Sicily beyond – and as rough a crossing on windy days as it was in Homer's Odyssey.

. . . There are moments of intense beauty at sea, often unexpected. It is not only the colour, the life, the gaiety of the unforgettable Cowes Week of 1975, perfect in every way except for the lack of wind on almost every day. It is not only the peace of eventide as the sun sets over the moorings at Burnham when the first touches of autumn appear. There is the beauty of the sea itself. Of all these scenes, the one which remains clearest in my mind was in the early morning of the last day of the Fastnet Race in August 1973. On deck, almost becalmed, I watched the sun gently rising through the low haze. Suddenly I realized I was seeing in colour for the first time what the Impressionists and those who followed them had seen. Between *Morning Cloud* and the sun the rippling sea was a multicoloured patchwork of brilliant yellows, purples and greens all dancing together. My mind leapt to Derain: he had just such a vision; he was able to convey it to others in paint. On the other side of *Morning Cloud*, out of the sun, everything was a smooth Whistlerian grey.

Sailing – A Course of My Life, Edward Heath

* * *

A ship swinging,
As the tide swings, up and down,
And men's voices singing,
   East away O! West away!
   And a very long way from London Town.

A lantern glowing
And the stars looking down,
And the sea smells blowing.
   East away O! West away!
   And a very long way from London Town.

Lights in wild weather
From a tavern window, old and brown,
And men singing together,
   East away O! West away!
   And a very long way from London Town.

A Sea Burden, C. Fox-Smith

* * *

Starting from Tower Pier in London, Francis Chichester sailed, with his wife Sheila and his son Giles as crew, to Plymouth, to the Royal Western Yacht Club's normal starting line off Plymouth Hoe. From there he sets sail alone on 'a sparkling sunny morning' to begin a single-handed voyage round the world, with only one stop. On his return, he is dubbed *Sir Francis* by Queen Elizabeth II with the sword believed to be the one used by Queen Elizabeth I to knight Sir Francis Drake:

Opposite page. Port Appin. Although steamers call here, port is a rather grand name for this sleepy little harbour in Argyll, Scotland. It lies between Loch Linnhe and Airds Bay.

September 17 brought my 65th birthday. I had a big time with a fresh-water wash, followed by opening Sheila's birthday present, a luxurious and most practical suit of silk pyjamas. I shed a tear to think of her kindness and love, and all the happiness we have had together since 1937. I started celebrating my birthday by drinking a bottle of wine given me by Monica Cooper and other members of our map-making firm for a birthday present. That was at lunch time. In the evening I wrote in my log:

'Well here I am, sitting in the cockpit with a champagne cocktail, and I have just toasted Sheila and Giles with my love. Full rig, *smoking*, smart new trousers, black shoes, etc. The only slip-up is that I left my bow-tie behind, and have had to use an ordinary black tie. I have carried this *smoking* (my green velvet designed and built by Scholte before I met Sheila in 1937) six times in *Gipsy Moth III* across the Atlantic, intending to dine in state one night, but this is the first time I have worn it in a *Gipsy Moth*. No dining in state, either. I don't get hungry in these 85°F heats until the middle of the night, or early morning. But why worry, with my bottle of the best presented by my own Yacht Club, the Royal Western Yacht Club, by that old satyr Terence (I always expect him to pull a pipe from some hidden pocket and start serenading Cupid), my dear Coz's brandy to make the cocktail, a lovely calm evening, hammering along at a quiet 7 knots on, extraordinary pleasure, a calm, nearly flat, sea. I will turn on some of the music Giles recorded for me. I meant to ask him to get a recording of Sheila and himself talking together, but forgot, which is not surprising, because the amount of thinking and planning for the voyage was unbelievable. A thousand items to remember or see to.

'This must be one of the greatest nights of my life – right in the middle of this wonderful venture – just passed by 100 miles the longest six-day run by any singlehander that I know of, and a great feeling of love and goodwill towards my family and friends. What does it matter if they are not here? I would not love them as I do in their absence, or at least I would not be aware of that, which seems to be what matters.

'People keep at me about my age. I suppose they think that I can beat age. I am not that foolish. Nobody, I am sure, can be more aware than I am that my time is limited. I don't think I can escape ageing, but why beef about it? Our only purpose in life, if we are able to say such a thing, is to put up the best performance we can – in anything, and only in doing so lies satisfaction in living.

'Is it a mistake to get too fond of people? It tears me to shreds when I think of Sheila and Giles being dead. On the other hand, I keep on thinking of the happiness and pleasure I have had at various times with them, usually when doing something with them. That first voyage home from America with Sheila, just the two of us, keeps on recurring to me, all the little episodes, and the joy and comradeship of it. The same with the third passage back, with Giles. I wonder if I shall ever enjoy anything as much. I see that action appears a necessary ingredient for deep feeling. This sort of venture that I am now on is a way of life for me. I am a poor thing, incomplete, unfulfilled without it.

Opposite page. Siphnos. On course for Faros, a small fishing harbour on this Greek island in the Aegean, some six hours' sail from Piraeus. Many of the island's 2,000 inhabitants are seafarers.

'It is too dark to see any more. Think of me – as the sky darkens, music playing, the perfect sail, and still half a bottle of the satyr's champagne to finish'.

Gipsy Moth Circles the World, Francis Chichester

The next morning at 2 a.m., Sir Francis wakes up with a hangover, when a sharp squall of wind lays *Gipsy Moth* on her side. The situation is serious because the companion is wide open – the sea could rush in and the boat founder. He is able to cope, slowly the boat rights itself and sails on.

'Would'st thou,' so the helmsman answered,
'Learn the secrets of the sea?
Only those who brave its dangers
Comprehend its mystery'.

High and Dry

Fitting out a boat, sorting out the charts, laying in stores . . . these are shore-based activities, while the ship rides at anchor or is high and dry. But for the sun-soaked super-rich, it is enough to enjoy the pleasures of yachting without ever leaving your moorings . . . after all, the sea can be quite rough!

* * *

The cork from a *Dom Perignon* bottle serves as a bung in the bottom of the dinghy on the stern of *Sundance d'Azur*. So this is why they told me that yacht chartering on the Riviera was 'champagne sailing'.

Sundance, a 70ft motor yacht moored at Antibes, is one of a giant multinational fleet that caters for an ever-growing band of landlubbers whose ideas of yachting often owe more to Errol Flynn than to Francis Chichester.

From St-Tropez to Monaco and beyond you can barely see the blue Mediterranean through the forest of masts, radar-scanners and whip-like aerials. In their docks and marinas the boats ride on a Technicolor porridge of diesel, empty bottles, plastic bags, beer cans and sometimes even seaweed. If ever all the vessels in this motley armada of mercenaries put to sea at the same time, the din of crunching plywood and smashing bottles would be heard in Lloyds of London.

Not that there is much fear of that ever happening. Life is much too comfortable when you are so conveniently connected by quayside umbilicals to fresh water, mains electricity and the telephone.

The Champagne Boat People, Alan Road (*Observer Magazine*)

* * *

How do you keep dry when you're at sea, with 'water water everywhere'? The perfect answer is yet to be found but they're working on it. And what sailors wear *ashore* is also serious business:

Foul-weather gear is supposed to keep you *dry*, and supplementary clothing should keep you warm and comfortable. But sailing always is a compromise and what you gain in one direction you loose in another. The dinghy sailor on a trapeze in cold weather has his mobility severely restricted if he wears foul-weather gear, sea boots, wool trousers, sweaters, wool cap, etc. For him, a wet suit that keeps him warm and comfortable, and does not restrict his mobility is a good choice.

Some foredeck men on ocean racers also favor the wet suit. But for the average offshore sailor, a wet suit is uncomfortable, hard to get into, and can raise a really good crop of salt water boils in a relatively short time.

Heavy, thick foul-weather gear that will practically stand by itself is not necessary when sailing in the summer. In such conditions you can use the good lightweight gear that is available on the market. Remember, though, that foul-weather gear material is waterproof to a certain PSI (pounds per square inch). Light gear may be waterproof if you are standing in a

rain squall or shower. But additional pressure compressed on the bottom of foul-weather gear when sitting, frequently causes leaking through the seat. Try it. Fill a shallow washtub with water six inches deep, put on your foul-weather trousers, and sit in the washtub with a good book and read for an hour. Then check the result.

If you really want to stay dry, the vast majority of offshore sailors, whether they be yachtsmen, professional delivery crews, or fishermen, are universal in their choice of a basic foul-weather-gear type of trousers held up by suspenders (braces to our British cousins) and a separate foul-weather jacket. The all-in-one foul-weather gear is popular primarily among dinghy sailors and inshore one-design racers.

I think it's essential for trousers to have a fly front. What is more discouraging than to be encased in foul-weather trousers, wool trousers, long winter woollies and suddenly you have to relieve yourself. Unless you have full-length hip boots under your foul-weather trousers (which allows relief between the boot and the foul-weather trousers) you simply must have a fly.

Seawise, Donald M. Street, Jr.

* * *

Fashion in naval dress is as varied as the design of ships. Just as exuberant carvings like the decoration of the *Royal Sovereign* of 1804 gave way to the functional severity of the modern vessel, so *Jack Spritsail's* gay stripes were eventually replaced by the sober dark blue of the lower deck uniform; and the waisted jacket. Close-fitting breeches and cocked hat of the officer, the dress prescribed by George II in 1747, was superseded by the flat peaked cap and straight-lined suit of today.

Common seamen wore what they pleased until uniformity was imposed in 1857. Before that time they often looked like pirates with ear-rings and stocking caps. They preferred short jackets long after the style had lapsed with landsmen; and they liked round straw hats, bright kerchiefs, bell-bottomed trousers, which were easy to roll up, and broad collars to protect their coats from the grease of their pigtails, which they continued to wear until the mid-19th century.

Olive Cook (*The Saturday Book*)

* * *

Men and women have always dreamed about the ships they are going to build and where they are going to sail in them. For many years it remains a dream but there are some for whom it comes true:

Within a few miles of my home in suburban Portland, Oregon, there are perhaps two dozen small ships — all sailing vessels of thirty to forty feet in length — in various stages of

Opposite page. St Malo. The most important seaport on the north coast of Brittany in France. From here in 1534 Jacques Cartier sailed forth to discover Canada — and in the 1980s deep-sea fishing boats still sail out into the Atlantic, for cod.

construction, with the ultimate purpose of carrying their owners and builders on world voyages.

The shipyards are old barns, backyards, temporary sheds of wood framing and plastic sheeting. Even at the small moorage on Multnomah Channel where I keep my sloop, there are four such vessels being built in a corner of the parking lot, and there is a waiting list for the space.

I am sure that similar activity can be found at every seaport of every maritime country in the Free World where the political, social, and economic status is sophisticated enough to stimulate the natural human urge to escape to a more simple life, or to indulge one's curiosity and restlessness by travel to faraway places.

And for every ship abuilding there are perhaps a thousand or more secret dreamers (many of whom live hundreds of miles from the nearest salt water) who spend their leisure hours marking ads in the classified sections of metropolitan newspapers and boating periodicals, or prowling the marinas, yacht clubs, and small boat harbors searching for a ship in which to make their escape at a price within their dreams.

Most of them, of course, will never get beyond the ad-marking stage; or if they do, most of their ardor will have been dissipated by the actual physical activity and the reality of inquiry. There is nothing new or unusual about this. Civilized man has endeavored to escape to sea at least since the time of the Minoans, circa 1500 B.C. Daydreams like this are what help many over the small daily crises, the frustrations of the job, and that state of mental rebellion that Henry David Thoreau was trying to define when he wrote that most men lead lives of quiet desperation.

Some of these owners, builders, and searchers have announced their intentions in advance, and are already savoring the heady stimulation of publicity and small notoriety which they hope to earn later. Others hold it as a secret ambition and will not talk about it, or if they do, they are vague about future ports of call and even departure dates. A few are building only what they refer to as 'retirement boats', for which they have no conscious plans other than living aboard when the ship is finished and launched. These are the cagey ones. They not only have the dream, but they have the means, the time and the personal discipline it takes to accomplish it. One has a feeling that they are waiting to see what the situation looks like when they are ready for sea, and chances are pretty good that one will learn at some future date that they are on their way around the world after all.

Among these dreamers is a bachelor and college professor who is completing his 32-foot Atkins ketch at precisely the same rate as his academic career draws to a close. When his boat is finished and his retirement checks are coming in regularly, he plans to sail the one hundred miles down the Willamette River of Oregon to the Columbia, and then down the ninety miles or so to the Pacific Ocean.

'When I get there,' he told me, *then* I will decide whether to turn right or left'.

The Circumnavigators, Donald Holm

Opposite page. Larnaca. On the south-east coast of Cyprus, Larnaca now has one of the biggest marinas on the island, jam-packed with boats resting-up or in for repairs.

Nowhere could be more high and dry than the place where the Norwegian anthropologist Thor Heyerdahl chose to build his boat – in the wilderness of the Sahara desert. In order to test the theory that the ancient Egyptians reached the Americas thousands of years before Colombus, Thor Heyerdahl planned to undertake the same voyage in a craft like the ones depicted on ancient tombs in Egypt, and built solely from materials that would have been available at the time:

A reed flutters in the wind.
   We break it off.
   It floats. It can bear a frog.
   Two hundred thousand reeds flutter in the wind. A whole meadow billows like a green cornfield along the shore.
   We cut it down. We tie it into sheaves, like great corn dollies. The bundles float. We go on board. A Russian, an African, a Mexican, an Egyptian, an American, an Italian, and myself, a Norwegian, with a monkey and a lot of clucking hens. We are off to America. We are in Egypt. It's blowing sand, it's dry and hot, it's the Sahara.
   Abdullah assures me that the reeds will float. I tell him that America is a long way off. He does not think people like black skins in America, but I assure him he is wrong. He does not know where America is, but we will get there in any case, if the wind is blowing that way. We will be safe on the reeds as long as the ropes hold. As long as the ropes hold, he says. Will the ropes hold?
   I felt someone shaking me by the shoulder and woke up. It was Abdullah. 'It's three o'clock,' he said. 'We are starting work again'. The sun was baking inside the hot tent canvas. I sat up and peered through a gap in the door opening. The dry heat and blinding sunshine of the Sahara thrust at me from outside. Sun, sun, sun. A sun-soaked expanse of sand met the bluest thing God has created, a cloudless desert sky unfolding in the afternoon sunshine above a world of golden-grey sand.
   A row of three large and two small pyramids were set like shark's teeth against the arch of sky. They had stood so, motionless and unchanging, since the time when men were part of nature and built in accord with nature. And in front of them, down in the shallow depression, lay something timeless, built yesterday, built ten thousand years ago, a boat in the desert sand, a sort of Noah's Ark stranded in the wilderness of the Sahara, far from surf and seaweed. Two camels stood beside it, chewing. What were they chewing? Trimmings from the boat itself perhaps, the 'paper boat'. It was built of papyrus. The golden reeds were lashed together in bundles, taking the form of a ship with prow and sternpost which stood out against the blue sky like a recumbent crescent moon.
   Abdullah was already on his way down there. And two coal-black Buduma Negroes in fluttering white robes were clambering on board, while Egyptians in colourful garments dragged up fresh bundles of papyrus reed. There was work to be done. 'Bot! Bot!' shouted Abdullah. 'More reeds!' I staggered out on to the hot sand as if I had awakened from a thousand-year sleep. After all, they were working for me; it was I who had conceived the absurd idea of reviving a boat-builder's art which the Pharaoh Cheops and his generation were

already beginning to abandon at the time when they ordered the building of those mighty pyramids which now stood there like a solid mountain range, hiding our timeless shipyard from the twentieth century maelstrom whirling in Cairo's hectic city streets down in the green Nile valley on the other side.

Our world, outside the tents, was bare sand. Hot sand, pyramids, more sand, and huge stacks of sun-dried reeds, brittle, combustible papyrus reeds, which the men were now dragging over to the liquorice-skinned Negroes who sat on the crescent moon, tightening rope lashings with the aid of hands, teeth and naked feet. They were building a boat – a papyrus boat. A *kadáy* they called it in their Buduma tongue, and they knew what they were building. Busy fingers and teeth strapped the loops round the reeds as only experts could. 'A paper-boat,' said the people at the Papyrus Institute down in the Nile Valley. For there they soaked these reeds in water and beat them into a crisp paper, to show tourists and scientists what the world's most ancient scholars had used to paint their hieroglyphic memoirs on.

A papyrus reed is a soft, sappy flower stem which a child can bend and crush. When it is dry it snaps like a matchstick and burns like paper. On the ground in front of me lay a tinder-dry papyrus reed, savagely screwed and fractured into a zigzag tangle. It had been thrown there in the morning by an indignant old Arab who mangled it between his fingers before flinging it away from him on the sand, spitting after it and pointing scornfully. 'That thing,' he said, 'that wouldn't even hold a nail; and how could you fix masts to a thing like that?' The old man was a canny boat-builder who had taken the bus up from Port Said to conclude a contract for masts and rigging for the vessel we were building. He was so outraged that he took the next bus back to the coast. Were we trying to make fun of an honest craftsman, or were the men of today completely ignorant of what was needed to build a decent craft? It was no good explaining to him that similar boats were painted in large numbers on the walls of the burial chambers of the ancient pyramid-builders out here in the desert. After all, these tombs also contain paintings of men with the heads of birds and serpents with wings. Anyone could see that a reed was a soft stalk in which neither nails nor screws could find a grip. Material for a haystack. A paper boat. Thanks for the return ticket.

The Ra Expeditions, Thor Heyerdahl

* * *

Thor Heyerdahl sailed 2,700 miles in *Ra I* before it was wrecked by a great storm and abandoned by the seven-man crew. A year later *Ra II* left Morocco, rounded the Canary Islands, off the NW coast of Africa, and crossed the Atlantic to the Caribbean. The possibility was established that ancient Egyptians, in a craft made mostly of papyrus, could have made a similar journey.

Unlike Thor Heyerdahl, Cecil Lewis was 'a designer of yachts who had never been to sea'. At the age of 71, he made up for it, sailing from Newhaven, on the south coast of England, to the Greek island of Corfu, in *Prosillos*, an untried 26-foot boat. The title of his book reflects his pragmatic approach – *Turn Right For Corfu*. Years before all that happened, Cecil Lewis, still a 'theoretical' sailor on dry land, revealed his remarkable instinctive feeling for boats, acquired through reading and thinking so much about them:

Piraeus. The chief port and bustling yacht marina of Greece, five miles from Athens.

I had been posted to command the R.A.F. staging post in Athens when we reoccupied Greece in 1944. My drawing board had been left behind in the U.K., but my mind was full of boats. We had a pretty tough time that winter when the Greek partisans turned on us and it was touch and go whether we should not be driven out of Greece altogether. But when the affair was over, one spring afternoon my adjutant and I took a jeep and pottered along the dirt road to the Bay of Salamis where the indomitable Greeks were already beginning to build replacements to the 10,000 caiques they had lost during the German occupation. The fascination of seeing wooden hulls take shape along the seashore in the open air, the smell of newly sawn wood, the primitive tools handled with much skill, all this, coupled with the fact that it was the first day of relaxation after an anxious time, sharpened all the senses and made everything imprint itself clearly on the mind. Suddenly I saw, moored about 100 yards offshore, the bare hull of a large yacht. She was stripped right down. Nothing but the hull remained and yet there was something about her lines, the way she sat on the water, the perfect proportion of her overhangs and, above all, the lilt of her sheer, that set my blood tingling as if I were listening to fine music. For to those who have not been caught by this particular form of beauty I should explain that, of all the lines in the design of a yacht, the most subtle, elusive and difficult to bring into harmony with the rest is the one that runs from the bow to the stern, the 'top' line of the boat – the sheer, as it is called. It is the line by which you can unfailingly recognise a designer when he has reached any eminence. Rhodes, Stevens, Fife, Clark: they all sign themselves by the sheer.

So there lay that lovely hull in the calm sunny waters of the Bay of Salamis, looking terribly forlorn and forgotten in the aftermath of war and I couldn't take my eyes off her. 'I'll bet my boots,' I said to my adjutant, who knew nothing about boats whatever, 'that boat's by Fife. It must be by Fife. Nobody else could draw that sheer. But what on earth is she doing here in Greece? How did she get here?' I stood rooted to the spot. She was very large. They didn't build them so big any more. There was only one hull by Fife that I knew, so large, so perfect – but it seemed impossible. And yet she must be, she was, *Suzanne*.

The picture (taken by Beken of Cowes) of *Suzanne* under full sail is one of the finest marine photos ever taken. I had first seen it in one of Uffa's* books and I see it still. It is the epitome of the pre-1st-war days of big sailing schooners, large crews and all the opulence and ease of an England now irrevocably gone. She is coming bustling down the Solent with the wind on her starboard quarter and everything she can carry set alow and aloft. She is all a-rustle with wind and foam and sunshine. 'Who wants to go to heaven,' I remember thinking, 'when they can have this here?'

I rushed down to the shore where a sailor was mending his nets and overwhelmed the poor man with questions that tumbled out of me in my excitement. 'What was that boat doing here? Who did she belong to? Was she for sale? What had happened to her masts, her sails, her gear? Was she British? What was her name?'

In his few words of English he managed to answer. 'Yes, British. She is *Suzanne*'.

Turn Right for Corfu, Cecil Lewis

*The English boat designer and builder, Sir Uffa Fox (1898-1972).

The world's first lifeboat was invented, not near the sea, but in the centre of London and by a man 'totally unconnected with the sea':

No one knows exactly the circumstances which led a fashionable coach-builder of Long Acre, named Lionel Lukin, to invent a Lifeboat.

Apparently his heart and mind had been stirred by the news that many lives were lost by the overturning of both rowing and sailing boats, and being a man of mechanical talent and inventive skill, he turned his attention to devise means for the prevention of such losses. But whence gained he the ideas of the use of cork and of air-cases for the safety of the boat?

He appears to have been totally unconnected with the sea. Perhaps this circumstance militated at first against the widespread recognition of his invention. 'What should a landlubber know of sailing craft?' seamen might not unnaturally have asked.

Possibly, too, there was something against him in the name he gave his boat. Greathead's craft was plainly called *The Lifeboat*, though we do not know who gave it the name; but Lukin dubbed his the *Unimmergible Boat*, and we suspect that comparatively few persons could in those days master the mysteries of such a title.

The writer of Lukin's obituary notice in the *Gentleman's Magazine* of 1834 shrewdly remarks that the importance of a name is generally too little considered; it is foolishly thought, says he, 'that the public is most attracted by Greek and grandiloquence;' but perhaps we may attribute Mr. Greathead's success to this circumstance, that, while Mr. Lukin's *Unimmergible Boat* seemed to demand some troublesome exercise of the understanding to comprehend its mysterious meaning, the title of 'The Lifeboat' spoke at once to the sympathies of the heart. It would be curious indeed if the difference of name caused the difference in the recognition of the inventors' claims . . .

His plan was this – he fixed to the yawl a projecting gunwale or upper rim of cork about nine inches thick amidships, and gradually sloped down to the stem and stern. Under this upper edge he placed double sides or air-tight enclosures, and also similar contrivances at the head and stern and under the seats. He added an iron keel by way of ballast, to keep the craft upright, while the hollow cases under the gunwale were believed to diminish rolling.

The boat seems to have been buoyant enough, but had apparently one defect, namely, the sides were liable to be staved in. No doubt the hollow air-cases under the upper edge contributed to this result, and Greathead's boat not having these side air-cases could not suffer from this defect.

But Lukin's boat was undoubtedly successful . . . in saving many lives for the first year it was at work. Lukin also had interviews with many influential persons, including Admirals King and Schank, the Dukes of Northumberland and Portland, and also with Lord Howe, First Lord of the Admiralty. Lord Howe gave him strong approbation verbally, but took no official steps to further the invention.

Opposite page. A lifeboat ready for a launch on a stretch of the east coast of England where violent seas and easterly gales are hazards to ships. It will be off and away within minutes of the maroons being fired.

A lifeboat on standby.

Paros. Rowing-boats bathed in the sunlight of the Aegean near a fishing village on this large Cyclodean island, some 100 miles from the mainland of Greece.

Lukin seems certainly to have done his best to spread abroad a knowledge of his invention, and appears unquestionably to have been the first in the field.

The Lifeboat, F. M. Holmes

* * *

The scene is a dinner at the Hotel Cecil in London on 2 July 1924. Among the guests are the Prince of Wales, later to become Edward VIII for a few months until his abdication in December 1936, Ramsay MacDonald, Prime Minister of Britain, and a clutch of Ambassadors. Winston Churchill was there too and is called upon to speak. He rises to his feet, a wisp of smoke curling up from the fat cigar resting on the ashtray in front of him:

Your Royal Highness, Your Excellencies, Mr Prime Minister, ladies and gentlemen . . . We live in a valiant age, an age which, although peculiarly a nervous age, nevertheless has proved capacities of daring, of self-abnegation, self-sacrifice, dauntless defiance to the brute powers of nature and of death, which no former age has excelled, which we may perhaps reasonably contend no former age has equalled; but there is something about the work of saving life which raises it, in certain aspects, above any form of peril and self-sacrifice which is combined with taking life. It is a great problem to balance the self-sacrifice of the soldier and the self-sacrifice of the Life-boatman. Still, one feels that the Life-boatman may plead that he represents the cause of humanity, and not that of any single nation or any single cause which may in the march of events from time to time arrive. (Cheers)

'Man the Life-boat!' – it is an inspiring call. It may, as the Spanish Ambassador has suggested to us, have other applications in daily life. When a friend is in trouble or in sickness 'Man the Life-boat!' If a class is submerged, ill-treated or exploited, 'Man the Life-boat!' If a small nation is fighting for its life, 'Man the Life-boat!' All these are applications of the same idea, but the finest of all is the simple actual sphere by the seashore. There is the glorious sphere of heroism and chivalry in human nature. The wreck lies on the reef, great waves are breaking over it, the timbers are going to pieces, the plates are buckling every hour, the crew and the passengers, women and children, are lashed to the rigging, clinging on to any coign of vantage which gives them shelter, or huddled in some structure which has survived the fury of the elements. There they are, out in the night, in the sea, in the tempest. They have no hope in this world except the Life-boat, but their signals have not been unperceived. The order has gone forth 'Man the Life-boat!' – an order which is never disobeyed. Great waves may thunder on the shore, winds may drive and beat with their utmost fury, the boat goes out, thrusts its way ahead to the wreck, it is twisted and turned by the convulsions of the sea, it is swamped with water, it is driven back, again and again it returns, it pursues and perseveres on its mission of rescue, of salvation, to those who are in peril, it drives on with a courage which is stronger than the storm, it drives on with a mercy which does not quail in the presence of

Opposite page. Granville. Smacks sheltering under the high walls by the harbour of this small seaport in Normandy, France, well-protected from the northern winds.

death, it drives on as a proof, a symbol, a testimony, that man is created in the image of God, and that valour and virtue have not perished in the British race. (Loud cheers.)

Winston Churchill, 2 July 1924

* * *

A ship was in distress in neighbouring Porlock Bay. A westerly gale was blowing at the time; high seas were sweeping across the front at Lynmouth and into the harbour. Under these circumstances, it was impossible for the lifeboat to put to sea. What then should they do? Give up all ideas of a rescue and let the sinking vessel die without making an attempt to take off her crew? Somebody had a better idea. If the boat was transported overland to Porlock, it should be possible to launch her.

It was, perhaps, a crazy suggestion, but there seemed to be no alternative. The distance was at least eleven miles, and all of it lay over rough country. The boat had to be transported from sea level to the clifftop (a height of 1,400 feet), and then down again. In places, the gradient was one in four-and-a-half. Banks had to be dug away to make the route wide enough; trees had to be sawn down; and gateposts removed. The whole thing was accomplished at night – with oil lamps, which were continually being blown out by the wind, as the only illumination. Aided by a band of voluntary helpers, it took the crew ten and a quarter hours before they reached the beach at Porlock. They were dead tired; and throughout the ordeal they had not paused to eat. Nor on their arrival was there time for a meal. They had to put to sea at once; but they reached their objective just in time. The crew of the helpless vessel were removed to safety minutes before she foundered.

Famous Rescues at Sea, Richard Garrett

* * *

Fishermen play an important part in helping to man lifeboats. One of the most famous was James Cable, born in 1851 at Aldeburgh on the Suffolk coast, where his father was lost at sea, his grandfather a member of the lifeboat's crew. James Cable served almost thirty years as coxswain of lifeboats and the new Aldeburgh lifeboat is named after him. Although James Cable devoted his life to rescue at sea, he remained, like Billy Burrell the present-day Aldeburgh coxswain, a fisherman; even on the morning of his wedding day he went out to get a good catch of cod:

In December, 1878, I was married to Emily Dyer, of Cowes, whose father was a gardener at Osborne House for forty years. On the morning of my marriage I went fishing and had a good catch of cod, but did not leave myself much time in which to prepare for church. My first son, Tom, was born the following year, and two years later James was born.

On that day the sea was exceedingly rough, and many people said I was foolish to take my boat out. However, I did, and within an hour made a record catch of sprats, quite close to the shore. When the other men on shore saw what a haul we were getting, seven more boats ventured. One of them capsized, but the men were saved. So heavy with fish was my boat that I had to anchor outside the shoal and signal to the men on shore to bring my other boat out to relieve me. I saw the second boat safely to shore, and then said I would stand by in case any of the others got into difficulty. Another of the boats with a heavy load shipped a lot of water and sank. We managed to get four of the men into my boat, and the other one was rescued by a boat launched from the shore. One old lady foolishly told my wife that I was in danger of being drowned, which upset her very badly in her condition; but she was all right when she saw me arrive safe and sound. There were sprats all along the beach: my catch was sixty-six bushels. I got £23 for it. The sunken boat, which was pulled in by the men on a rope, had forty bushels of sprats in it.

A Lifeboatman's Days, James Cable

* * *

H. E. Bates tells another fisherman's tale. This happened in 1940 when the curtain was coming down on a world that would never reappear in quite the same form, the last of the days when fish was cheap:

Down on the harbour-quay at Folkestone the smacks used to lie close in under the steep walls, copper sails flagged in the shelter of the harbour, light fawn-gold nets slung out on the drying poles in the sun, swinging like curtains, lobster-pots stacked here and there on the fish-smeared flag-stones or piled under the low railway arches over which the boat-trains ran into the port. Whenever you went there it seemed the fish was just in. It was in the boats and they were piling it into bath-tins and bringing it ashore up the steps; or it was already ashore and it lay everywhere, if it was a good catch, on the concrete floor of the market, in tins and boxes or baskets, silvery, bloody, still leaping, orange-spotted plaice, halibut, dog-fish, cod, soles, mackerel, herring, oceans of silver sprats, with the gulls screaming and diving above; or the auctioneer was already selling it to a crowd that never seemed to be listening but only gazing heavily at the wet concrete where the dog-fish were still panting and leaping and the turbot looked like solid marble; or it was already sold and they were skinning the dog-fish and packing the boxes for the trains and the old men were already baiting the lines for another trip and the hawkers already piling the fish into lumps on the barrows standing between the chandler's store and the mission hall. 'Sixpence a lump lady, where you like'.

H. E. Bates, *(The Saturday Book)*

* * *

From 1928 to 1937, Evelyn Waugh, who wrote several famous books, including *Brideshead Revisited*, had no fixed home and no possessions which would 'not go conveniently on a porter's barrow'. At that time, for a young man with a modest amount of money, 'the going was good' and Evelyn Waugh sailed as a passenger on the *Stella Polaris*, a Norwegian-owned 6,000-ton motor yacht. It docked in the Bay of Naples early on a Sunday morning and Evelyn Waugh goes ashore:

By the time that we had finished breakfast, all the formalities of passport and quarantine offices were over, and we were free to go on shore when we liked. A number of English ladies

went off in a body, carrying prayer-books, in search of the Protestant church. They were outrageously cheated by their cab driver, they complained later, who drove them circuitously and charged them 85 lire. He had also suggested that instead of going to matins they should visit some Pompeian dances. I, too, was persecuted in a precisely similar way. As soon as I landed a small man in a straw hat ran to greet me, with evident cordiality. He had a brown, very cheerful face, and an engaging smile.

'Hullo, yes, you sir. Good morning,' he cried. 'You wanta one nice woman'.

I said, 'no, not quite as early in the day as that'.

'Well, then, you wanta see Pompeian dances. Glass house. All-a-girls naked. Vair artistic, vair smutty, vair French'.

I still said no, and he went on to suggest other diversions rarely associated with Sunday morning. In this way we walked the length of the quay as far as the cab rank at the harbour entrance. Here I took a small carriage. The pimp attempted to climb on to the box, but was roughly repulsed by the driver. I told him to drive me to the cathedral, but he took me instead to a house of evil character.

'In there,' said the driver, 'Pompeian dances'.

'No,' I said, 'the cathedral'.

The driver shrugged his shoulders. When we reached the cathedral the fare was 8 lire, but the supplement showed 35. I was out of practice in travelling, and after an altercation in which I tried to make all the wrong points I paid him and went into the cathedral. It was full of worshippers. One of them detached himself from his prayers and came over to where I was standing.

'After the Mass. You wanta come see Pompeian dances?'

I shook my head in Protestant aloofness.

'Fine girls?'

I looked away. He shrugged his shoulders, crossed himself, and relapsed into devotion . . .

At dinner that evening at the Captain's table the lady next to me said, 'Oh, Mr Waugh, the custodian at the museum was telling me about some very interesting old Pompeian dances which are still performed, apparently. I couldn't quite follow all he said, but they sounded well worth seeing. I was wondering whether you would care to . . .'

When the Going was Good, Evelyn Waugh

* * *

When you're an attractive young woman just about to make a single-handed dash across the Atlantic in the 38-foot *Robertson's Golly*, the media make a dead set at you. On board, making final preparations for a transatlantic race, Clare Francis gives in to the demands of a persistent photographer, until her French friend, Jacques, sends him on his way:

Most photographers were happy with the inevitable coil of rope, but on one occasion I allowed

Opposite page. Paphos. The fishing harbour, a focal point on the west coast of Cyprus, is ringed by tavernas serving the day's catch of exotic fish, including swordfish, squid, octopus and mullet.

myself to be pressurized into wearing a bikini. I was unhappy about it – after all, they don't ask Harvey Smith to pose on his horse in bathing trunks – but the photographer was obstinate and I thought it easier to give in and get it over with quickly. As I posed shivering beside the mast I suddenly noticed the photographer looking nervously behind him. 'Do you have a dog aboard?' he asked. Not as far as I knew, I replied. 'Then what's that growling?' he demanded.

The growling noise got louder and soon emerged from the main hatch in the form of Jacques, his teeth bared in a menacing snarl. I stepped hastily between him and the photographer. 'What,' he asked menacingly, 'has the photograph to do with sailing the Atlantic?'

'Now, darling . . .' I began soothingly.

'Does this twit really imagine you dress like that to pull up the mainsail?'

'Well, no . . .'

'What does he think this is . . . the *Playboy*!'

The photographer was retreating steadily down the deck, looking anxiously for an escape route. Jacques, his English exhausted, strode after him breathing torrents of what was undoubtedly very rude French.

Come Hell or High Water, Clare Francis

* * *

Edward Heath sails in the grand manner, as befits a former Prime Minister of Great Britain. His favourite drink is champagne, as befits a former leader of the Conservative Party. This combination makes him ideally qualified to advise on the tricky business of launching a ship.

You can only be sure of success in this specialized field of launching ships by taking a firm grip of the bottle with one hand on the neck and the other on the base and then hurling it as violently as possible at your objective!

Sailing – A Course of My Life, Edward Heath

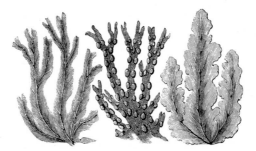

Opposite page. Cannes. The smartest resort on the Côte d'Azur in the south of France, a luxurious retreat for millionaires' yachts and of the so-called 'champagne boat people'.

Ol' Man River

The sea is grandiose and impersonal. But rivers, because they have a continuous relationship with the land on either side, are mostly more sociable, enigmatic and intimate: after all, you can even have a river at the bottom of your garden. We battle with the sea, contend with it and challenge it: but with rivers, we try to make friends and understand them, because rivers can be complex and perverse:

> Ol' man river, dat ol' man river,
> He must know sumpin', but don't say nothin',
> He just keeps rollin',
> He just keeps rollin' along.

Showboat, Oscar Hammerstein II

* * *

'I'm going to take a sixteen-foot boat down the river to New Orleans and the Gulf of Mexico,' I said. 'At least, that's what I was going to do.'

'Sixteen feet? That's a pretty good size of boat. You won't have too much trouble at all. I seen guys go down the Mississippi in all kinds of things. Twelve-foot jonboats . . . canoes . . . why, just a month or two back, we had two crazies go through here in a pedal boat like they have in parks. They thought they was going to New Orleans.'

The thought of the two men in the pedal boat took the glory out of my own trip at a stroke.

'Did they make it?'

'I never heard nothing of them since.'

I had, after all, dreamed of disappearing from the world. 'Went down the Mississippi, never heard of since,' would at least make a tantalising line on a modest memorial slab somewhere.

'Oh, you'll have problems. You get down in some of the big pools, like the Dubuque pool — that's one of the worst pools, is the Dubuque pool. She's wide open: four, five miles, as far as you can see. There's stump lines . . . When you're not there . . . boy, when it gets rough it can really get rough in a hurry. Then you'll get wakes. When some of them big tows get down in the flats, they're pushing along at ten, twelve miles an hour, and they'll turn the whole river to a rooster tail.'

'What do I do then?'

'You stay right inshore and ride those waves out. If you're in the channel, you'll be running into waves that are seven feet tall. Even up here, we've had boats tipped over, just from wakes. We get drownings every day. You going to ride the Mississippi, you better respect her or she'll do you in.'

His lock basin had filled. It had the absolute stillness of the moment after the last note of

Opposite page. The Po. Tow-rope on the bank of Italy's longest river (420 miles), flowing through Turin, chief city of Piedmont, across Lombardy and out to the Adriatic.

the finale before the applause begins. He ran his eye along the brimming surface. I felt that the lockmaster was a kindred spirit, a man who simply loved water. He softened every time that he looked at his pet element, his long, chipped, hatchet-face taking on a moony other-worldliness.

'But you've got to watch that sky. You ever see anything queer about it, if the clouds look wrong somehow, you get off the river. Oh, you'll see thunder and lightning. Hell, you could run into a hurricane. There's storms on the Mississippi so bad even the big tows get lost sometimes. There's tows gone down there, just sucked under in a storm on the river. She can be meaner than the ocean. But you'll be okay. Just remember, if there's something in the air that don't feel right, *get off the river*. You'll get to know her. You'll learn the signs. The time you got to start worrying is when she goes dead quiet. That's when she means to get up to something, and that's when you get off that river.'

Old Glory, Jonathan Raban

* * *

Between Iffley and Oxford is the most difficult bit of the river I know. You want to be born on that bit of water, to understand it. I have been over it a fairish number of times, but I have never been able to get the hang of it. The man who could row a straight course from Oxford to Iffley ought to be able to live comfortably, under one roof, with his wife, his mother-in-law, his eldest sister, and the old servant who was in the family when he was a baby.

Three Men in a Boat, Jerome K. Jerome

* * *

So on thy banks, too, Isis,* have I strayed
A tasselled student, witness you who shared
My morning walk, my ramble at high noon,
My evening voyage, an unskilful sail
To Godstow bound, or some inferior port,
For strawberries and cream. What have we found
In life's austerer hours delectable
As the long day so loitered?

Robert Southey

* *Isis*, the name of an Egyptian nature goddess, is the name given to a stretch of the Thames flowing through Oxford.

* * *

Dark brown is the river,
Golden is the sand,
It flows along for ever,
With trees on either hand.

A Child's Garden of Verses, Robert Louis Stevenson

One of the most famous river events in the world is the annual Oxford and Cambridge Boat Race. Thousands crowd the banks of the Thames to watch and millions more, all over the world, get a better if less involved view on television. The first Boat Race took place in 1829. One of the most extraordinary was the Boat Race of 1877, described by the magazine *Punch* in four bewildering words: 'Oxford won – Cambridge too!' By good fortune, an Oxford undergraduate, Lewis Farnell, was watching on the towpath, near Barnes Bridge, and left us this account of the race, in which victory belonged to neither Oxford nor Cambridge – but to chivalry:

As they came through the bridge I saw to my joy Oxford going rapidly ahead and daylight appearing for the first time between the boats; normally Oxford should have won by at least two lengths. But suddenly Oxford staggered and stood still in a mass of foam: the bow-oar, Cowles, had struck the top of a big wave in feathering and broken his blade clean off: before our boat could recover from the shock, Cambridge drew up level. Then Grenfell, now Lord Desborough, rowing four, shouted 'row on': Oxford started again with seven oars, and in the last three-quarters of a mile beat Cambridge fairly by nearly a third of a length. It was so obvious, that the Dark Blue flag was immediately hoisted on high, and the news was wired round England that Oxford had won: and every man in the Cambridge boat knew it and admitted it; and in our joy we pushed each other into the water. The only person who had not seen it was the umpire, old John Phelps, who had never seen a near race before, and lost his head, and shut his eyes, and merely maintained that 'He could not tell who had won'. Therefore the two Presidents decided that it must be called a dead heat; and though Cambridge chivalrously offered the victory to Oxford, the latter with still greater chivalry declined to accept it. For some time after it became a joke in the music-halls, to talk of a 'dead heat by ten yards'. This was the most thrilling sporting experience of my life; and what I saw and have here narrated was confirmed by Cowles, the innocent cause of what was technically a loss but virtually a greater triumph, when I met him some thirty years afterwards.

* * *

Britain has a Queen on the throne and a woman Prime Minister in charge of the Government, so it was only a matter of time before Cambridge or Oxford shattered tradition by having a *woman* cox in the Boat Race crew. The Oxford University Boat Club was the first to open the doors, of what had been an exclusively male preserve for over a century and a half, to a woman – and Susan Brown entered the pages of history:

The Boat Race has had its share of the good, the bad and the indifferent when it comes to coxing, and played an important role in the development of the art of steering in two-boat races generally. The most recent, most notable coxswain to meet fate on a fine day and 'to get a blue; at any rate to be quite famous' is Miss Susan Brown of Honiton in Devon and Wadham College, Oxford. This slight, dark-haired, mellow-complexioned student of biochemistry became the first woman to steer in the men's Boat Race in 1981, at the invitation of the president, Chris Mahoney. She learned to cox at Wadham and became a member of the British

women's training team, eventually going to the Moscow Olympic Games. They were coached by Oxford's coach Dan Topolski, so he spotted her talents early in her steering career, much of it spent with the women on the Tideway. She was twenty-two, very softly spoken, purposeful, yet slipping about on the bank almost unseen. She was a nightmare for the reporters because she had very little to say to their repetitive trite questions about women's lib, diet, making history, had she got a boyfriend in the crew, and so on. She was a nightmare for the broadcasters for similar reasons, and when she did say something they couldn't hear her. She was a dream for the photographers because, without resorting to the gimmickry of showing her legs or wearing tight singlets, she looked like a revelation in every picture taken. For the first three months of 1981 Sue Brown must have passed before more shutters than anyone except for Lady Diana Spencer. Miss Brown was the tousled girl next door enjoying the fresh air and the good fortune to be engaged by the blues; Lady Diana was the enchanting salon smasher, engaged to the heir to the throne. They could never have swopped places, but for a while they both filled the papers. The crew got angry at times. Soon after Brown's blue boat seat was announced one of the oarsmen at a Radley practice session yelled, 'Go back to Lady Diana, you vultures'.

The Oxford & Cambridge Boat Race, Christopher Dodd

* * *

1839, ten years after the first Oxford and Cambridge Boat Race, was the year of the first Regatta at Henley, between Oxford and London. The Henley Royal Regatta is now established as one of the great world events in the rowing calendar. In those early years, Warrington Wilkinson Smyth, a Cambridge undergraduate, in an eight-oar boat, the *Black Prince*, carried off the Grand Challenge Cup at Henley and the crew rowed up to London to celebrate.

The young Queen Victoria was at the beginning of her long reign and we retreat for a moment from our world of computers, jet-lag and the 'Star Wars' defence programme to the gentle peaceful world of early Victorian England, the world that everyone thought would go on for ever:

On the following morning, Saturday, 15 June, Smyth awoke at the Red Lion from a confused consideration of eight oars, medals, gunfirings and silver cups, and packed all his moveables into his hatbox. A hearty breakfast and involved calculations over the bill delayed the *Black Prince's* departure until almost midday, when with the cup in its box in the bows, and amid flag-waving and cheering from the bridge, the men from First Trinity pulled out for London. Their hearts were lighter, though some heads were heavier, than on the previous day as they moved along the reach for the last time, and they were delayed by a huge West Country barge at Hambledon Lock. They passed the ruins of Medmenham Abbey, embowered in trees, and passed under a suspension bridge at Marlow, where a good-looking church was under

Opposite page. Oxford. An old College Barge on the Isis, the busiest stretch of the river, where summer 'eights' are rowed and where the Oxford oarsmen train for the great annual Boat Race with Cambridge.

construction, and saw a model of a frigate lying off someone's lawn at Maidenhead. They walked up to the great castle at Windsor and then visited the chapel at Eton, reminiscent of that of their near neighbour at Cambridge, King's. They passed Magna Charter Island and the bow end of the boat had violent cachinnations about the beauty or otherwise of the tower of Egham church, and they paddled past many little villas and spent the night at a waterside inn at Thames Ditton.

Here Wythe and Gough bribed the chambermaid to let them lie in on the following morning, delaying embarkation by an hour. Looking round as he toiled steadily at his oar, plash plashing in the bright morning sunlight, Smyth was astonished at the beauty of Richmond while Barclay craned his neck to steer a passage through the multitude of craft pleasuring about. The *Black Prince* carried her silver cup proudly past the Duke of Northumberland's Sion House, a most ungainly lump of architecture, Smyth thought. From Kew they had a tedious paddle at low water to Putney, where they disembarked to visit Mrs Avis, who had put up Smyth and Penrose with the Cambridge crew for the Boat Race. She produced champagne to drink to the cup and then filled it with flowers for them.

Henley Royal Regatta, Christopher Dodd

* * *

When the American wit, Robert Benchley, first arrived in Venice, he cabled home: 'STREETS FULL OF WATER – PLEASE ADVISE.' The last stage of the journey to Venice for everything and everybody is in a *vaporetto* (the Venetian water-bus), a water-taxi, a gondola or some other of the bewildering variety of water transport that weaves its way through the 170-odd canals of that watery city:

And among them all, the very image of Venice, straight-descended from Carpaccio, moves the gondolier. He is not a popular figure among the tourists, who think his prices high and his manner sometimes overbearing: and indeed he is frequently a Communist, and no respecter of persons, and he often shamelessly pumps the innocent foreigner with inaccurate information, and sometimes unfairly induces him to disregard the tariff ('Ah, but today is the feast of San Marcuola, *signor*, and it is *traditional* to charge double fares on this holy day'). I have grown to like and admire him, though, and I can forgive a few peccadillos among men who live on a four-months' tourist season, and scrape the winter through as part-time fishermen and odd-job workers. The gondoliers are usually highly intelligent: they are also tolerant, sardonic, and, with some grumpy and usually elderly exceptions, humorous. They are often very good-looking, too, fair and loose-limbed – and many of their forebears came from the Slav coasts of Istria and Dalmatia – and they sometimes have a cultivated, worldly look to them, like undergraduates punting on the Cherwell, naval officers amusing themselves, or perhaps fashionable ski instructors . . .

Opposite page. Venice. The gondola is the 'hansom cab' of Venice, graceful, silent, wildly expensive, propelled with lordly flourishes by its gondolier, the undisputed aristocrat of Venetian waterways.

Now and then they have regattas, partly impelled by the power of tradition, partly by the Tourist Office. In many a smoky *trattoria* you will see, carefully preserved behind glass, the trophies and banners of a regatta champion, or even his portrait in oils — it is customary to commission one: and there is still a lingering trace of popular enthusiasm to these races, a faint anthropological echo of folk rivalries and ancestral feuds. Fiercely and intently the competitors, sweat-bands to match their colourful oars, pound down the Grand Canal, or swing around the marker buoy beside the Public Gardens. A raggle-taggle fleet of small craft follows their progress, speedboats and rowing-boats and tumble-down skiffs, half-naked boys in canoes, big market barges, elegant launches, yachts, all tumbling hilariously along beside the gondolas, with their ferry steamers swerving precariously towards the quay, and a fine surge of foam and clatter of engines, as in some nightmare University Boat Race, half-way to a lunatic Putney.

Venice, James Morris

* * *

A barge can denote different kinds of vessels. At one extreme, the ceremonial barges of the Doges of Venice were amongst the most splendid and magnificent boats ever built. Shakespeare described the barge that Cleopatra, Queen of Egypt, rode in as 'like a burnished throne, with the poop of beaten gold and oars of silver'. At the bottom end of the market are the heavy-going, clumsy, basic flat-bottomed freight barges, carting cargo along rivers and canals.

Handling a long unresponsive barge on a narrow river is no joke: bargemen are tough uncompromising watermen given to speaking their minds:

For centuries the Thames lighter or dumb barge has made use of the tides to provide the cheapest possible form of water transport, and in essentials the hull has remained unchanged until present times, when newer streamlined designs have been introduced, better adapted to towing than propulsion by oars. A long, flat-bottomed, boxlike structure, with sloping ends, called for the minimum skill in construction, and was capable of being controlled by one man handling one or two sweeps, or long oars. That worthy has two missions in life. The first is to keep his unwieldy craft in the best run of the tide, and the second to reply in equally fluent language to all the pleasant (?) remarks hurled at him by every other user of the river. I can assure the reader that even today a lighterman standing on his rights — and he has many by reason of ancient charters — is well worth listening to for variety of expression and choice of words, so that it is difficult to know how they justify the name, dumb barge! Any reference to offspring related to a canine quadruped of the female gender immediately calls for repartee of the most robust kind, and a really fluent master of the art of invective will seldom repeat himself so long as he remains in hearing. I remember seeing a dumb barge, propelled by a brawny fellow, start to cross the George V dock, just as a P. & O. liner was moving out in charge of tugs. The tortoise-like crawl of the lighter was only equalled by the seething impatience of the irate tug master, who had a voice like a foghorn, and must have easily been heard on the other side of the river, and the waterman was anything but dumb.

'To swear like a bargee' is an expression, which to my mind, is a libel on the splendid men who handle sailing barges, although at times, when justifiably incensed, like everyone else, they give vent to their feelings in no uncertain way. This reminds me of the story of the week-end yachtsman who was getting under weigh in a most unseamanlike manner. Immaculate in white flannels, with a natty cap worn at a Beatty angle, he would not have disgraced the Castle lawns at Cowes, but he knew little of the profession he aspired to follow. Gradually he drifted down across the hawse of an anchored spreetie and bumped along her low sides. On seeing the master coming up the companionway to investigate the cause of the strange sounds the resplendent one said:

'Excuse me, sir, all I can say is I'm awfully sorry'.

The bargeman was in his shirt sleeves and dirty from much wrestling with the stove flues. He took his pipe from his mouth, spat over the side, and replied witheringly:

'H'm! Is that all you can say? Well, now you listen to me, and maybe you'll l'arn summat'.

Fortunately, I am able to give some particulars of the part played by sailing barges in the early days of the cement industry, as I had the pleasure of meeting Captain Charles Inge, age 83, now living in retirement at Halling, where many long-lived barges were built in the past, so evidently there is something in the air there which induces longevity. He told me that he started bargeing at the early age of 13, going as third hand with his father in the *Alice*, a 44-ton round-bowed topsail barge, built at Faversham in 1859, and still carrying cement in the 1920's, when she was owned by the A.P.C.M. In those far-off days in the 'seventies, she belonged to Hilton's of Faversham, who later joined in the firm of Brooks, and in 1900 amalgamated with the A.P.C.M. His first trip was from Halling to Faversham with chalk, and for three winters they went down Swin to Harwich to load Roman stone for the Kentish port. When in command of *Dee* some years ago, Capt. Inge saw the last of this old barge *Alice*, lying at Blackwall Point with her stern off, evidently having been run down after a long and useful life.

His first rise was when he went as mate in *Richard,* a 35-ton stumpie barge, built at Chiswick in 1867. Tiller steered, she carried a bowsprit and jib, but the spar was more trouble than it was worth, as there was little room for'ard of the windlass for rigging it out and the sail was a job to stow, so after a few trips it was done away with. *Richard* was a narrow barge, only 14ft beam, to enable her to pass through the locks at Brentford. The usual trip was lime from Halling to Brentford, 74 miles, which included shooting 18 bridges, much use of the setting boom and rowing from Woolwich. Sometimes a horse towed them in the upper reaches, and in those days meadows and open country lined the banks of the Thames. One of the first tugs to be available for towing was *Wanderer*, a converted yacht, 'all glass', to use Captain Inge's own words, and her services were utilised if available. The return cargo was coke from Fulham to the Medway cement works.

Primitive though these methods may seem to modern eyes, used to the hurry of motor lorries, some smart times were recorded, an average trip from the Medway was three tides, and when one considers the laborious task of rowing a heavy barge for 23½ miles, one gets an idea how hard a bargeman's life was in those days.

Spritsail Barges of Thames and Medway, Edgar J. March

The Loire. The Ol' Man River of France, the country's longest river (600 miles), crossed by Joan of Arc in 1429 to relieve the great siege of Orleans.

Long before the days of mechanical power, when the wind dropped, barges were hauled along waterways by teams of men, scrambling along banks and wading through shallows. Later, horses took over this gruelling work, plodding heavily and uncomplaining along the towpaths, providing one of the cheapest forms of locomotion. Journeys were long and slow, so often the bargeman, his wife and children would live on board and the horse would be treated like one of the family:

On the Regent's Canal, recesses with grooved ramps can still be seen which were built to help horses climb out if they fell in, the idea being that the horse would walk along the bottom till he came to a ramp where he would be coaxed to climb out.

Generally, it was not too difficult to get a horse out of the canal (which was about 3 foot 6 inches deep); you knew that another boat containing some able assistance was guaranteed to come round the corner within the next five minutes, and also, the towpaths were lined with telegraph poles. The procedure was to fit a block and tackle to the top of a telegraph pole, get the horse near to the bank, and lever him upwards with a plank under his belly, using a pile of stones for a pivot. Having been lifted so far, the block and tackle would be used to keep the horse high while he was swung onto the bank.

The old generation of boatman, in particular, treated his horse very well; always making sure that he was stabled, fed and made comfortable for the night before he would go into his cabin or the pub. Stables were sometimes provided by locks, or at pubs. When the towing horse could not be stabled, he was tethered on the bank by the boat. The horse was always regularly groomed, 'till 'e shone like glass', and some canal horses won prizes at local shows for the best turned-out horse.

The boatman would make sure the horse's collar was warm and dry before he put it on – as he would with his own socks. Along with the rest of the boat, the horse shared an array of brasses and had his own brightly painted horse-bowl and colourful bobbins. Sometimes each bobbin was painted a different colour, others would be painted in four colours like a barber's pole. Even the wife did not forget the poor old horse, and crocheted him a pair of ear-caps to keep the flies off in summer.

The Narrow Boat Book, Tom Chaplin

* * *

Bradshaw's Canals and Navigable Rivers of England and Wales used to be the 'Bible' of anyone travelling on those waterways. This 'Handbook of Inland Navigation for Manufacturers, Merchants, Traders and Others' became a classic work of extraordinary diligence, detail and accuracy. Henry Rodolph de Salis, who compiled it, wrote *every* page from his own personal knowledge, which he acquired by spending eleven years exploring 14,000 miles of rivers and canals:

Examples of a large number of locks per mile are 58 in 16 miles between Worcester and Tardebigge on the Worcester and Birmingham Canal, in which are included the famous flight of 30 at Tardebigge, which is the greatest number in one flight in the United Kingdom.

There are also 74 locks in 20 miles between Huddersfield and Ashton on the Huddersfield Narrow Canal, and 92 in 32 miles between Manchester and Sowerby Bridge on the Rochdale Canal.

The largest canal lock in the United Kingdom is the large entrance lock to the Manchester Ship Canal at Eastham, which measures 600ft by 80ft. In passing, it may be mentioned that the Lady Windsor Lock of Barry Docks is supposed to be the largest and deepest of any lock in the world, it measures 647ft long, 65ft wide, and is 59½ft deep from quay wall to invert. The smallest locks in use in the country for trade are the nine locks on the Old Shropshire Canal between Wappenshall Junction and Trench, referred to above, and which pass boats measuring 70ft by 6ft 2in.

Locks, as a rule, are not constructed to give a greater fall each than from 6 to 8 feet, as otherwise they would use an excessive amount of water, and the bottom gates would become of abnormal size. Excluding for the moment the locks of the Manchester Ship Canal, the single canal lock having the greatest fall in the country, so far as the Author has observed, is No 6 lock from Merthyr Tydfil on the Glamorganshire Canal, which has a fall of 14ft 6in. Tardebigge top lock on the Worcester and Birmingham Canal would appear to come next with a fall of 14ft. Three of the Manchester Ship Canal locks, however, have falls in excess of the above, namely Latchford, Irlam, and Barton, the falls of which are respectively 16ft 6in, 16ft, and 15ft.

The provision of an adequate supply of water to canals is often an expensive matter. Each time a vessel passes through a summit level or highest pound of a canal it consumes two locks of water, that is to say, a lock full at each end, which has to be replaced, but which amount of water will, theoretically at any rate, suffice for working all the locks for the passage of that vessel below the highest lock on each side of the summit level. To maintain the supply of water to the summit level of a canal impounding reservoirs are generally provided to store the rainfall from as large an area as possible for use as required, the supply from the reservoirs being often supplemented by pumping from wells and from streams where available.

Bradshaw's Canals and Navigable Rivers of England and Wales,
Rodolph de Salis

* * *

The waters of the world are sovereign Powers. We may pollute them, dam them or divert them, but they remain beyond our degradation. They are better and older than us. John Burns the radical was right, when he called the Thames *liquid 'istory*. Many a politician, withdrawing to the Commons terrace or the Kennedy Center balcony from the heady puerilities of debate, must have been sobered into wiser judgement by the dark calm flow of the river below, and there are places in the world where this partnership of the water, at once aesthetic and functional, sets the whole tone of a society, and gives it the particular steady assurance that goes with an organic purpose.

Take, for example, the Mississippi. Abraham Lincoln thought it the most powerful force on earth, and certainly its progress through the American South is masterful more than slavish. Its yellowish muddy motion there, and the endless traffic of the river-craft through its shoals

and cut-offs, still dictates the character of the country along its banks; and nothing in travel is more satisfying than to leave your car in a cotton-field of Arkansas or Tennessee, scramble to the ridge of the dusty levee, and discover the great river there at your feet, with the long line of a tow thudding its way to Vicksburg or New Orleans – the radar twirling on its wheelhouse, the sun glinting on its paintwork, and the off-duty crew stripped to the virile waist with mugs of coffee around the galley door.

Or think of a city like Singapore. It is not the most beautiful of towns, but because of the water that is its *raison d'être*, it is one of the most formidable. It was built to a purpose, designed for a trade, and it lives by the sea. Its prospect is the Strait, looking across to Sumatra and the archipelago, and littered with tangled melancholy islands. Its promenade is the waterfront, intermittently dressed up with esplanades and monuments, but in essence a working quay. Everywhere the sea seeps through Singapore, in canals and backwaters and crowded wharfs, and always in the roadsteads lie the ships that are its familiars – opulent tankers from the west – shambled coasters from the island trade – junks, dhows, Malay schooners, warships – and all those myriad bum-boats, ferry-boats, rafts, punts, lighters and antique company launches which seem, in all such Oriental water-cities, never actually to have been constructed, but simply to have been washed up and encrusted on the land's edge, like oysters.

Travels, Jan Morris

Opposite page. Henley-on-Thames. The first Boat Race between Oxford and Cambridge was held here in 1829. But Henley is famous now for the Royal Regatta, started in 1839, and now held yearly in July.

Business in Great Waters

They that go down to the sea in ships,
That do business in great waters;
These see the works of the LORD,
And his wonders in the deep.

Psalm 107

* * *

The seas of the world are arenas of big business, like the City of London and Wall Street. Go into the great fish markets and you will see changing hands – pounds, dollars, Deutschmarks, lire, yen and all the other currencies, as the harvests of the seas are bought and sold. Look in on Lloyd's Register of Shipping in London or downtown New York and you will find big deals aplenty in progress. Everywhere in all the great ports, loading and unloading of millions of tons of cargo never ceases; and without supertankers on the sea-lanes, the wheels of the world would stop turning.

Exploration, research, biology and even anthropology are pursued on and beneath the surface of the oceans. The sea has provided some of the most portentous of battlefields, from the two greatest seafights in English history: the defeat of the Spanish Armada in 1588 and Nelson's victory at Trafalgar in 1805, to the political demonstration in Boston harbour in 1773, known forever after, in one of history's understatements, as the Boston Tea Party. In 1982, with a touch of Drake and Nelson and flag-waving galore, another armada set sail – the Task Force to the Falkland Islands in the South Atlantic.

Away from the billowing black smoke and the carnage of battle, the sea can be a fun-fair, or an expensive shimmering playground for the rich. James Morris looks at the scene in New York harbour one summer and then takes a walk from Fifth Avenue to the Hudson piers:

Thousands of New Yorkers take to the boats for pleasure. Any fine day, April to November, the yachtsmen sail in their armadas into the sheltered waters around the Bay – one of the most astonishing sights of the affluent society. It is still smart, of course, to own a boat. In the Hudson River there sometimes lie yachts of legendary luxury ('floor-to-floor wheelhouse carpeting', as a harbor policeman once put it to me), and in the boat basin at the west end of 79th Street movie actors and Greek millionaires often bask in their yachts among Old Masters and young mistresses, rather than subject themselves to the discomforts of a penthouse suite at the Plaza. I was told of a film producer who used his yacht to move about Manhattan, as others might take a taxi: a fellow guest at a dinner party one night, offered a lift home to his apartment a few blocks away, found himself conveyed by sea from the East Side to the West Side of Manhattan, via Battery Point.

. . . I ended my walk in a ship chandler's, a shop remote indeed from the delights of Saks or Bonwit Teller, but hardly less seductive. No crested appointment to royalty, I thought, could be grander than this establishment's credentials: *Purveyors of Ship's Stores since the Days of the Sailing Ships*. Tiffany or Abercrombie and Fitch never sold objects more alluring than the binnacles, chronometers, toggles, tarpaulins, and radar screens on display there, and I doubt if Parke-Bernet ever auctioned finer titles than these: *Hints for Master Mariners, The Bluejacket's Manual, Questions and Answers for Third Mates*. I always enjoy the suavity of a really sophisticated shop assistant's approach, inquiring if you would care to have the Tang horses taken out of their cabinet, or try the mink on, but I know no grander opening gambit than the one I overheard in the chandler's that day:

'When you sailin', captain?'

The Great Port – A Passage Through New York, James Morris

* * *

Many ships are equipped with laundries, but where such services are not available the following hints will be of value for the washing, care and maintenance of it.

When electric irons are provided they should be treated with the utmost care. Irons should be repaired only by an authorized person of the electrical branch. Any defects resulting from mis-use are chargeable to the mess or rating responsible. If a flat-iron is not available quite good results can be obtained with the loom of an oar or a rolling pin.

In fine weather washed clothing is hung to dry on the clothes lines provided for the purpose, and normally from after working hours until sunset. At the pipe 'Up washed clothes' clothing is securely stopped to the lines with no 'holidays' (i.e. gaps) between separate articles. The lines are then triced up out of reach. On the pipe 'Down washed clothes' the lines are lowered and each rating is responsible for collecting his own clothing.

The Naval Ratings Handbook, 1938 (British Admiralty)

* * *

It is fantastic to be, at the same time, Prime Minister of Great Britain and captain of the British team in one of the foremost ocean racing contests in the world. Each job, separately, demands all the time, stamina and availability that could be expected from one person.

Edward Heath managed both. It began for him in 1966 when one weekend he took some sailing lessons at Broadstairs, an old-fashioned seaside resort on the Channel coast. Three years later he won the tough Sydney to Hobart race in the first *Morning Cloud*.

In 1970 the Conservative Party won the General Election and Edward Heath became Prime Minister. The following year he skippered the British team that regained the Admiral's Cup, an international contest in which each country enters a team of their three fastest yachts. Inevitably there were conflicts of duties and interests:

When I had the talks with President Pompidou in Paris in May 1971 which led to the successful conclusion of the negotiations for Britain's entry into the European Community, we had both planned that the meeting would end with the lunch which the French President would attend at the British Embassy on the second day, a Friday.

I was then to fly home, travel down to *Morning Cloud* and sail in the Channel Race that evening. But at lunchtime we found we could make much greater progress than we had expected so we decided to carry on with the talks. My private secretary sent a message to *Morning Cloud* to sail without me.

That evening, when all had been settled, President Pompidou said to me:

'Well, you have missed your race. A fortnight ago you won. What do you want to happen this time? Is it better for them to win without you, in which case it will show you don't matter, or not to win, in which case *Morning Cloud* has lost an important race just before your Admiral's Cup trials? Which is it to be?'

There was nothing I could do either way. *Morning Cloud* settled it by coming second!

Sailing — A Course of My Life, Edward Heath

* * *

Sea shanties (shanty comes from the French *chanter*, 'to sing') were working songs, chanted or sung while men were doing jobs on board, like stomping round the capstan to haul up the anchor chain, or hoisting sails. Some collectors of these old songs think they are as pure as driven snow. But anyone who has had a spell of unwilling chastity knows how sexual fantasies come to the surface when men are singing together and can colour the most innocent words with erotic innuendoes.

You can read what you like into the words of *So Handy Me Gels*, sung long ago by sailors to co-ordinate the rhythm of pulling on the halyards, the ropes that hoisted the spars up the masts of the square-rigger, carrying aloft the heavy sails:

> So handy me gels, so handy!
> Why can't you be so handy O?
> Handy me gels, so handy!
> For we are outward bound you know.
> Handy me gels, so handy!
> For we are outward bound you know.
> Handy me gels, so handy!
>
> Be handy with your washing, girls,
> Because my love's a dandy, O.
> Handy me gels, so handy!
>
> My love she is a dandy, O,
> And she is fond of brandy, O,
> Handy me gels, so handy!
>
> O shake her up and away we'll go,
> Up aloft from down below.
> Handy me gels, so handy!
> Be handy.

The practice of whistling is discouraged in H.M. ships because the noise is apt to be confused

Larnaca. The new port of this important city on the south-east coast of Cyprus.

with the piping of orders. It is usually anything but sweet, except in the ears of the perpetrator, and is more often than not a cause of annoyance to his messmates.

The Naval Ratings Handbook, 1938 (British Admiralty)

* * *

In the Black Ball Line I served my time –
    Away-ay-ay, Hooray-Ah.
And that's the line where you can shine,
    Hooraw for the Black Ball line . . .

And now we're bound for New York Town –
    Away-ay-ay, Hooray-Ah.
It's there we'll drink and sorrow drown.
    Hooraw for the Black Ball line.

* * *

Three short accounts of moments at sea. The first is by Edward Lacey as he says farewell to England; in the second, Charles Darwin reluctantly submits to the 'crossing the line' ceremony; and in the third, George Mackay Brown describes how, in a storm at sea, an Orkney fisherman pulls out all the stops to get help from the Almighty:

Saturday May 31 1862. Turned out at 6 a.m. and walked the poop for two hours before breakfast. A fine day and we met several homeward bound vessels; our first Saturday night at sea. We are now on the Devonshire coast about 14 miles from the land. The passengers and crew are on deck watching the sun go down, making a superb panorama view, while the ship is gliding along at 8 knots like a swan without any perceptible movement. The water is smooth and the sun setting behind the hills looks like a sheet of gold. It is a magnificent sight, as if England knew we were taking our last look at her and wished to display herself in all her glory. Night has now hidden her from our view. We heave a deep sigh and go below to think of those we are are leaving behind.

(From an account of the voyage of the *Orient* from London to Adelaide, written by Edward Lacey.)

Diaries from the Days of Sail, edited by R. C. Bell

* * *

We have crossed the Equator, and I have undergone the disagreeable operation of being shaved. About nine o'clock this morning we poor 'griffins', two and thirty in number, were put all together on the lower deck. The hatchways were battened down, so we were in the dark and very hot. Presently, four of Neptune's constables came to us and one by one led us up on deck. I was the first and escaped easily: I nevertheless found this watery ordeal sufficiently disagreeable. Before coming up, the constable blindfolded me and, thus led along, buckets of water were thundered all around. I was then placed on a plank, which could be easily tilted up into a large bath of water. They then lathered my face and mouth with pitch and paint, and scraped some of it off with a piece of roughened iron hoop: a signal being given, I was tilted head over heels into the water, where two men received me and ducked me. At last, glad enough, I escaped: most of the others were treated much worse, dirty mixtures being put in their mouths and rubbed in their faces. The whole ship was a shower-bath, and water was flying about in every direction. Of course not one person, even the Captain, got clear of being wet through . . .

The Voyage of the Beagle, Charles Darwin

* * *

'We'd do weel to pray,' said a North Ronaldsay fisherman to his crew as another huge wave broke over them.

It had been a fine day when they launched the boat. Then this sudden gale got up.

Willag was a kirk elder. The skipper told him to start praying.

Spindrift lashed in and over.

'O Lord,' said Willag, 'Thou are just, thou art wonderful, Thou art merciful, great are Thy words, Thou art mighty'. Willag faltered in his litany of praise.

The boat wallowed through a huge trough.

'Butter Him up!' cried the skipper. 'Butter Him up!'

An Orkney Tapestry, George Mackay Brown

* * *

Pirates were the gangsters of the high seas, plundering vessels in the same way that highwaymen held up coaches. They operated especially in the West Indies, off the Atlantic Coast of America and, right up to the 19th century, in the Mediterranean. These rough ruthless sea rovers showed little mercy to their victims and Jonathan Swift has left us this blow-by-blow account of what it was like to be accosted by a ship flying the pirate's flag, the *Jolly Roger*:

We had not sailed above three days, when a great storm arising, we were driven five days to the north-north-east, and then to the east; after which we had fair weather, but still with a pretty strong gale from the west. Upon the tenth day we were chased by two pirates, who soon overtook us; for my sloop was so deep loaden, that she sailed very slow, neither were we in a condition to defend ourselves.

We were boarded about the same time by both the pirates, who entered furiously at the head of their men, but finding us all prostrate upon our faces (for so I gave order) they pinioned us with strong ropes, and setting a guard upon us, went to search the sloop.

I observed among them a Dutchman, who seemed to be of some authority, though he was not commander of either ship. He knew us by our countenances to be Englishmen, and jabbering to us in his own language, swore we should be tied back to back, and thrown into the sea. I spoke Dutch tolerably well; I told him who we were, and begged him in consideration of our being Christians and Protestants, of neighbouring countries, in strict

alliance that he would move the Captains to take some pity on us. This inflamed his rage; he repeated his threatenings, and turning to his companions, spoke with great vehemence, in the Japanese language, as I suppose, often using the word *Christianos*.

The largest of the two pirate ships was commanded by a Japanese Captain, who spoke a little Dutch, but very imperfectly. He came up to me, and after several questions, which I answered in great humility, he said we should not die. I made the Captain a very low bow, and then turning to the Dutchman, said, I was sorry to find more mercy in a heathen, than in a brother Christian.

Gulliver's Travels, Jonathan Swift

* * *

A raft is built of nine balsa-wood logs. The longest, laid in the middle, is 45-foot and shorter ones are arranged along both sides. The logs are held together with thick hemp rope, without using a single spike, nail or any plaited wire. In the middle, slightly aft of centre, a tiny open cabin is built out of bamboo canes and reeds. Power comes from a rectangular 'square sail' hoisted up on two masts cut from hard mangrove wood. That hardly sounds like a vessel in which six men should attempt to cross the South Pacific. But they did.

In 1947 the Norwegian anthropologist, Thor Heyerdahl, set out to prove that people from ancient civilisations in South America could have made the crossing to the Polynesian Islands in the South Pacific in the only vessels that would have been available to them – balsa-wood rafts:

When the sea was not too rough we were often out in the little rubber dinghy taking photographs. I shall not forget the first time the sea was so calm that two men felt like putting the balloon-like little thing into the water and going for a row. They had hardly got clear of the raft when they dropped the little oars and sat roaring with laughter. And as the swell lifted them away and they disappeared and reappeared among the seas, they laughed so loud every time they caught a glimpse of us that their voices rang out over the desolate Pacific. We looked round us with mixed feelings and saw nothing comic but our own hirsute bearded faces; but as the two in the dinghy should be accustomed to those by now, we began to have a lurking suspicion that they had suddenly gone mad. Sunstroke, perhaps. The two fellows could hardly scramble back on board the *Kon-Tiki* for sheer laughter, and gasping, with tears in their eyes, beg us just to go and see for ourselves.

Two of us jumped down into the dancing rubber dinghy, and were caught by a sea which lifted us clear. Immediately we sat down with a bump and roared with laughter. We had to scramble back on to the raft as quickly as possible and calm the two last who had not been out yet, for they thought we had all gone stark staring mad.

It was ourselves and our proud vessel which made such a completely hopeless, lunatic impression on us the first time we saw the whole thing at a distance. We had never before had

Opposite page. Seriphos. A fishing boat tethered in Leivadi, the small harbour of this tranquil island on the Cyclades, some 80 miles from the mainland of Greece.

91

an outside view of ourselves in the open sea. The logs of timber disappeared behind the smallest waves, and when we saw anything at all it was the low cabin with the wide doorway and the bristly roof of leaves that bobbed up from among the seas. The raft looked exactly like an old Norwegian hay-loft lying helpless, drifting about in the open sea, a warped hay-loft full of sunburnt bearded ruffians. If anyone had come paddling after us at sea in a bath we should have felt the same spontaneous urge to laughter. Even an ordinary swell rolled halfway up the cabin wall and looked as if it must pour in unhindered through the wide open door in which the bearded fellows lay gaping. But then the crazy craft came up on the surface again and the vagabonds lay there as dry, shaggy and intact as before. If a higher sea came racing by, cabin and sail and the whole mast might disappear behind the mountain of water, but just as certainly the cabin with its vagabonds would be there again next moment.

It looked bad, and we could not realise that things had gone so well on board the peculiar craft.

The Kon-Tiki Expedition, Thor Heyerdahl

* * *

In a more conventional craft, Hilaire Belloc experiences the 'terror and salvation, happy living, air, danger, exultation, glory' of going to sea in a little boat:

Certainly every man that goes to sea in a little boat of this kind learns terror and salvation, happy living, air, danger, exultation, glory, and repose at the end; and they are not words to him, but, on the contrary, realities which will afterwards throughout his life give the mere words a full meaning. And for this experiment there lies at our feet, I say, the Channel.

It is the most marvellous sea in the world – the most suited for these little adventures; it is crammed with strange towns, differing one from the other; it has two opposite people upon either side, and hills and varying climates, and the hundred shapes and colours of the earth, here rocks, there sand, here cliffs, and there marshy shores. It is a little world. And what is more, it is a kind of inland sea.

People will not understand how narrow it is, crossing it hurriedly in great steamships; nor will they make it a home for pleasure unless they are rich and can have great boats; yet they should, for on its water lies the best stage for playing out the old drama by which the soul of a healthy man is kept alive. For instance, listen to this story:

The sea being calm, and the wind hot, uncertain, and light from the east, leaving oily gaps on the water, and continually drying down, I drifted one morning in the strong ebb to the South Goodwin Lightship, wondering what to do. There was a haze over the land and over the sea, and through the haze great ships a long way off showed, one or two of them, like oblong targets which one fires at with guns. They hardly moved in spite of all their canvas set, there was so little breeze. So I drifted in the slow ebb past the South Goodwin, and I thought: 'What is all this drifting and doing nothing? Let us play the fool, and see if there are no adventures left'.

So I put my little boat about until the wind took her from forward, such as it was, and she crawled out to sea.

It was a dull, uneasy morning, hot and silent, and the wind, I say, was hardly a wind, and most of the time the sails flapped uselessly.

But after eleven o'clock the wind first rose, and then shifted a little, and then blew light but steady; and then at last she heeled and the water spoke under her bows, and still she heeled and ran, until in the haze I could see no more land; but even so far out there were no seas, for the light full breeze was with the tide, the tide ebbing out as strong and silent as a man in anger, down the hidden parallel valleys of the narrow sea. And I held this little wind till about two o'clock, when I drank wine and ate bread and meat at the tiller, for I had them by me, and just afterwards, still through a thick haze of heat, I saw Grisnez, a huge ghost, right up against and above me; and I wondered, for I had crossed the Channel, now for the first time, and knew now what it felt like to see new land.

Hills and the Sea, Hilaire Belloc

* * *

But a single-handed passage in a small sailing boat is about the most expensive way of crossing the Atlantic known to man. True, one can be penniless and lucky in some old boat held together by hope, and potter down through the trade winds to the West Indies, do some island hopping, and hope ultimately to make New York. But that was not what Francis [Chichester] wanted: he did not want to potter, he wanted to race. And he did not want the easy run of a trade wind passage: he wanted to drive himself and his boat more or less across the Great Circle route direct from Plymouth to New York, knowing that on an east-west crossing he would have the currents of the Gulf Stream against him all the time, and a chance of headwinds for much of the time. This sort of passage cannot be attempted in an old boat held together by hope.

J. R. L. Anderson, in *The Guardian*

* * *

I also felt like lunch, and I had a splendid lunch, eating the last lettuce given me by Nancy, which was excellent with a crushed garlic clove. One advantage of the Atlantic is that one can eat as much garlic and onion as one likes, and I like a lot. I had smoked salmon first, but it was too salt, packed in brine, with Danish Blue cheese, and gingerbread to follow. I made a blunder here; I didn't have Stilton as I had last time; Stilton just has that extra something. I had dates and raisins in my salad and, of course, a *Mackeson* stout to start with, and *Whitbread* pale ale to go on with. The *tout ensemble* would be hard to beat.

Atlantic Adventure, Francis Chichester.

* * *

A century before Jacques Yves Cousteau brought back for our television screens pictures of the exotic, translucent and intensely beautiful world under the sea, Jules Verne, the first science fiction writer, described with astonishing accuracy the brilliant iridescence of submarine landscapes. Here he is in 1870 on the seabed of the Pacific Ocean – in his imagination:

The light, which lit the soil thirty feet below the surface of the ocean, astonished me by its power. The solar rays shone through the watery mass easily, and dissipated all colour, and I clearly distinguished objects at a distance of a hundred and fifty yards. Beyond that the tints darkened into fine gradations of ultramarine, and faded into vague obscurity. Truly this water which surrounded me was but another air, denser than the terrestrial atmosphere, but almost as transparent. Above me was the calm surface of the sea. We were walking on fine even sand, not wrinkled, as on a flat shore, which retains the impression of the billows. This dazzling carpet, really a reflector, repelled the rays of the sun with wonderful intensity, which accounted for the vibration which penetrated every atom of liquid. Shall I be believed when I say that, at the depth of thirty feet, I could see as if I was in broad daylight?

For a quarter of an hour I trod on this sand, sown with the impalpable dust of shells. The hull of the *Nautilus*, resembling a long shoal, disappeared by degrees; but its lantern, when darkness should overtake us in the waters, would help to guide us on board by its distinct rays.

Soon forms of objects outlined in the distance were discernible. I recognized magnificent rocks, hung with a tapestry of zoophytes of the most beautiful kind, and I was at first struck by the peculiar effect of this medium.

It was then ten in the morning; the rays of the sun struck the surface of the waves at rather an oblique angle, and at the touch of their light, decomposed by refraction as through a prism, flowers, rocks, plants, shells and polypi were shaded at the edges by the seven solar colours. It was marvellous, a feast for the eyes, this complication of coloured tints, a perfect kaleidoscope of green, yellow, red, orange, violet, indigo and blue; in one word, the whole palette of an enthusiastic colourist! . . .

Various kinds of isis, clusters of pure tuft-coral, prickly fungi and anemones, formed a brilliant garden of flowers, enamelled with porphitae, decked with their collarettes of blue tentacles, sea-stars studding the sandy bottom, together with asterophytons like fine lace embroidered by the hands of naiads, whose festoons were waved by the gentle undulations caused by our walk. It was a real grief to me to crush under my feet the brilliant specimens of molluscs which strewed the ground by thousands, of hammerheads, donaciae (veritable bounding shells), of staircases, and red helmet shells, angel-wings and many others produced by this inexhaustible ocean.

20,000 Leagues Under the Sea, Jules Verne

* * *

In *Henry V*, Shakespeare has left us the most stirring description ever written of a battle squadron at sea. 'Fair stood the wind for France' as the royal fleet embarks to fight for 'Harry! England and Saint George!'

> Thus with imagined wing our swift scene flies,
> In motion of no less celerity
> Than that of thought. Suppose that you have seen
> The well-appointed king at Hampton pier

Zea. Immaculate yachts berthed at Zea, the crowded yacht marina near Piraeus, Greece.

Embark his royalty; and his brave fleet
With silken streamers the young Phoebus fanning:
Play with your fancies, and in them behold
Upon the hempen tackle ship-boys climbing;
Hear the shrill whistle which doth order give
To sounds confused; behold the threaden sails,
Borne with the invisible and creeping wind,
Draw the huge bottoms through the furrow'd sea,
Breasting the lofty surge: O, do but think
You stand upon the rivage and behold
A city on the inconstant billows dancing;
For so appears this fleet majestical,
Holding due course to Harfleur. Follow, follow!
Grapple your minds to sternage of this navy;
And leave your England, as dead midnight still,
Guarded with grandsires, babies and old women,
Either past or not arrived to pith and puissance;
For who is he, whose chin is but enrich'd
With one appearing hair, that will not follow
These cull'd and choice-drawn cavaliers to France?

Henry V, William Shakespeare

* * *

Nearly four centuries after Henry V's expedition, Britain is again at war with France. Midshipman Horatio Hornblower faces the challenge of boarding a small boat from a frigate, as ship and boat pitch together in a rough sea:

'Mr Hornblower!'
'Sir!'
'Take four men of the cutter's crew and board that brig. Mr Soames will give you our position. Take her into any English port you can make, and report there for orders'.
'Aye aye, sir'.
Hornblower was at his station at the starboard quarterdeck carronades — which was perhaps how he had caught Pellew's eye — his dirk at his side and a pistol in his belt. It was a moment for fast thinking, for anyone could see Pellew's impatience. With the *Indefatigable* cleared for action, his sea chest would be part of the surgeon's operating table down below, so that there was no chance of getting anything out of it. He would have to leave just as he was. The cutter was even now clawing up to a position on the *Indefatigable's* quarter, so he ran to the ship's side and hailed her, trying to make his voice sound as big and as manly as he could, and at the word of the lieutenant in command she turned her bows in towards the frigate.
'Here's our latitude and longitude, Mr Hornblower,' said Soames, the master, handing a scrap of paper to him.

'Thank you.' said Hornblower, shoving it into his pocket.

He scrambled awkwardly into the mizzen-chains and looked down into the cutter. Ship and boat were pitching together, almost bows on to the sea, and the distance between them looked appallingly great; the bearded seaman standing in the bows could only just reach up to the chains with his long boat-hook. Hornblower hesitated for a long second; he knew he was ungainly and awkward – book learning was of no use when it came to jumping into a boat – but he had to make the leap, for Pellew was fuming behind him and the eyes of the boat's crew and of the whole ship's company were on him. Better to jump and hurt himself, better to jump and make an exhibition of himself, than to delay the ship. Waiting was certain failure, while he still had a choice if he jumped.

Perhaps at a word from Pellew the *Indefatigable's* helmsman allowed the ship's head to fall off from the sea a little. A somewhat diagonal wave lifted the *Indefatigable's* stern and then passed on, so that the cutter's bows rose as the ship's stern sank a trifle. Hornblower braced himself and leaped. His feet reached the gunwale and he tottered there for one indescribable second. A seaman grabbed the breast of his jacket and he fell forward rather than backward. Not even the stout arm of the seaman, fully extended, could hold him up, and he pitched headforemost, legs in the air, upon the hands on the second thwart. He cannoned onto their bodies, knocking the breath out of his own against their muscular shoulders, and finally struggled into an upright position.

'I'm sorry.' he gasped to the men who had broken his fall.

'Never you mind, sir.' said the nearest one, a real tarry sailor, tattooed and pigtailed. 'You're only a featherweight'.

'Would you go to the brig, please, sir?' he asked the lieutenant in command who was looking at him from the sternsheets. The lieutenant bawled an order and the cutter swung round as Hornblower made his way aft.

It was a pleasant surprise not to be received with the broad grins of tolerantly concealed amusement. Boarding a small boat from a big frigate in even a moderate sea was no easy matter; probably every man on board had arrived headfirst at some time or other, and it was not in the tradition of the service, as understood in the *Indefatigable*, to laugh at a man who did his best without shirking.

Midshipman Hornblower, C. S. Forester

* * *

Steam-power locomotion for ships first led to the paddle-steamer equipped with large wheels on either side and long paddles projecting at right angles from them. Before very long, of course, the rotating propellor, the *screw*, took over, but in the meantime it was the paddle-steamers that broke records: the *Britannia*, racing across the Atlantic at 8 knots on her first crossing in 1840, wasted no time in claiming the Blue Riband for the fastest crossing. A few years later British-built paddle-steamers played a curious role in the American Civil War:

During the American Civil War of 1861-5 another breed of paddle steamer appeared on the Atlantic. In April 1861 the Northern States declared a blockade of the southern ports in an

attempt to starve the Confederates of arms and supplies. The blockade also had the effect of depriving the Lancashire cotton industry of its raw materials, so when Confederate agents began to arrive in British ports looking for fast steamers to run the blockade, they found no shortage of willing agents.

The Confederates needed ships which were fast enough to outrun the warships of the blockading squadrons, and the fast cross-channel steamers which were then so common in British waters fitted the bill perfectly. Many such ships were sold and converted to run the blockade, and soon found themselves dodging enemy warships in the waters between Bermuda, the Bahamas and the American coast. As ships were captured or sunk by the Northern gunboats, the supply of spare cross-channel vessels began to run out, and several British yards began to build vessels specifically as blockade runners. One of the best-known builders' yards was that of Messrs. Jones, Quiggin & Company, of Liverpool, who produced such famous ships as the *Banshee* of 1862, and the infamous *Colonel Lamb* of 1864, which caused the Union a great deal of worry both as a successful blockade runner and as a privateer. By the time the blockade was lifted in 1865, most of the fast steamers had either been destroyed or captured and commissioned in the U.S. Navy. One or two, including the *Colonel Lamb* returned to commercial service, or were sold to foreign navies.

Paddle Steamers, Richard Clammer

* * *

What does it feel like to be the Admiral in command of the major proportion of the French Fleet, including their two finest modern battle-cruisers, the *Dunkerque* and the *Strasbourg*, and to read this message delivered by a British officer:

'It is impossible for us, your comrades up to now, to allow your fine ships to fall into the power of the German or Italian enemy. We are determined to fight on to the end, and if we win, as we think we shall, we shall never forget that France was our ally, that our interests are the same as hers and that our common enemy is Germany. Should we conquer we solemnly declare that we shall restore the greatness and territory of France. For this purpose, we must make sure that the best ships of the French Navy are not used against us by the common foe. In these circumstances, His Majesty's Government have instructed me to demand that the French Fleet now at Mers-El-Kebir and Oran shall act in accordance with one of the following alternatives:

'(a) Sail with us and continue to fight for victory against the Germans and Italians.

'(b) Sail with reduced crews under our control to a British port. The reduced crews will be repatriated at the earliest moment.

'If either of these courses is adopted by you, we will restore your ships to France at the conclusion of the war or pay full compensation, if they are damaged meanwhile.

'(c) Alternatively, if you feel bound to stipulate that your ships should not be used against

Opposite page. Lampedusa. A long narrow island, stretched out from east to west, some nine hours' sail from Porto Empedocle on the south coast of Sicily.

the Germans or Italians unless these break the Armistice, then sail them with us with reduced crews, to some French port in the West Indies, Martinique, for instance, where they can be demilitarized to our satisfaction or be perhaps entrusted to the United States and remain safe until the end of the war, the crews being repatriated.

'If you refuse these fair offers, I must, with profound regret, require you to sink your ships within six hours . . .'

France signed an armistice with Germany on 22 June 1940. Britain was vitally concerned about the future of the French battle-cruisers, destroyers and submarines, which lay at adjacent ports on the Northern African shore of Morocco.

Winston Churchill takes up the melancholy story in a speech to the House of Commons, July 4, 1940:

'We had hoped that one or other of the alternatives which we presented would have been accepted, without the necessity of using the terrible force of a British battle squadron . . . However, no doubt in obedience to the orders dictated by the Germans from Wiesbaden, where the Franco-German Armistice Commission is in session, Admiral Gensoul refused to comply and announced his intention of fighting.

'Admiral Somerville was, therefore, ordered to complete his mission before darkness fell, and at 5.53 p.m. he opened fire upon this powerful French Fleet . . .

'A large proportion of the French Fleet has, therefore, passed into our hands or has been put out of action or otherwise withheld from Germany . . .

'I leave the judgment of our action, with confidence, to Parliament. I leave it to the nation, and I leave it to the United States. I leave it to the world and history'.

> *The War Speeches of the Rt. Hon. Winston S. Churchill*, (compiled by Charles Eade)

* * *

Splicing the main brace means an extra issue of a tot of rum, or an issue of lemonade (to officers and men under twenty and any who prefer it). This is only authorised on some special occasion of celebration.

> *The Naval Ratings Handbook*, 1938 (British Admiralty)

* * *

The following extract contains a brilliant 'technicolour' account by Lt-Commander Robert Hichens of an engagement with the enemy in the second World War:

On the 1st August 1942, four British gunboats set out from Dartmouth on a typical anti-E boat patrol. Just off Cherbourg they found four E-boats in line ahead and scarcely moving, probably awaiting permission to enter harbour . . . The Germans were completely and utterly taken by surprise, while the gunboats slowly circled them, raking them with fire. Then the enemy began to wake up. Here is Hichens' own description of what followed:

Gare de l'Arsenal. Boats can tie up right in the centre of Paris, in this strip of water near the Seine.

Shore batteries began to sing by, bursting with brilliant effect. The sight was unforgettable. Pale yellow-green luminosity from the slowly dropping shower of starshells, fierce red, green and yellow streaks of tracer interlacing in fantastic patterns, vivid splodges of light where the big shells were bursting; roar of engines, crash and stutter of guns; the almost silent, motionless line of E-boats, glittering white in the artificial radiance and seemingly strangely helpless in their immobility; the dark line of the breakwater spitting bright flashes of flame irregularly, viciously, up and down the line, like a crazed xylophonist striking his keys wantonly and at random; the cautiously approaching towering hulls of the two torpedo boats lit brightly by the occasional bursts of our 2-pounder shells on their sides, still obviously puzzled, but the flashes from their guns gaining in momentum as they closed; the line of gunboats weaving and storming round their quarry, still magnificently together in tight line-ahead formation, the spray thrown back at 24 knots reflecting the green effulgence of the staryshells in a luminous halo round the hulls. 'It was', he comments, 'no time for losing oneself in the wild beauty of the scene'.

The Battle of the Narrow Seas, Peter Scott

* * *

The Cruel Sea by Nicholas Monsarrat has been called 'one of the best books ever written about the sea'. Monsarrat once said that the men are the stars of his story, the only heroines are the ships and the only villain – the sea:

Compass Rose turned under full helm, and raced for her second attack. This time it was simpler: perhaps they had done some damage after all, because the U-boat did not seem to be moving or making any attempt at evasion. 'Target stationary, sir!' reported Lockhart as they complete their turn, and he repeated the words, at intervals, right down to the very end of their run-in. Once more the depth-charges went down, once more the enormous crack of the explosion shook the whole ship, once more they waited for success or failure to crown their efforts.

Someone on the bridge said: 'Any minute now . . .'

The U-boat rose in their wake like a huge unwieldly fish, black and gleaming in the sunlight.

A great roar went up from the men on the upper deck, a howl of triumph. The U-boat came up bows first at an extraordinary angle, blown right out of her proper trim by the force of the. explosion: clearly she was, for the moment beyond control. The water sluiced and poured from her casings as she rose: great bubbles burst round her conning-tower: gouts of oil spread outwards from the crushed plating amidships. 'Open fire!' shouted Ericson – and for a few moments it was Baker's chance, and his alone: the two-pounder pom-pom, set just behind the funnel, was the only gun that could be brought to bear. The staccato force of its firing shook the still air, and with a noise and a chain of shock like the punch! punch! punch! of a triphammer, the red glowing tracer-shells began to chase each other across the water towards the U-boat. She had now fallen back on a level keel, and for the moment she rode at her proper trim: it was odd, and infinitely disgusting, suddenly to see this wicked object, the loathsome cause of a hundred nights of fear and disaster, so close to them, so innocently exposed. It was like seeing some criminal, who had outraged honour and society, and had long been shunned, taking his ease at one's own fireside.

The two-pounder was beginning to score hits: bright flashes came from the U-boat's bows, and small yellow mushrooms of cordite-smoke followed them: the shells were light, but the repeated blows were ripping through her pressure-hull and finding her vitals. As *Compass Rose* came round again, listing sharply under her full helm, the machine-guns on her bridge and her signal-deck joined in, with an immense clatter. The U-boat settled a little lower, and men began to clamber and pour out of her conning-tower. Most of them ran forward, stumbling over the uneven deck, their hands above their heads, waving and shouting at *Compass Rose*; but one man, more angry or more valiant than the rest, opened fire with a small gun from the shelter of the conning-tower, and a spatter of machine-gun bullets hit *Compass Rose* amidships. Then the counter-firing ceased suddenly, as the brave man with the gun slumped forward over the edge of the conning-tower; the rest of the crew started jumping overboard – or falling, for *Compass Rose's* guns were still blazing away and scoring hits on men and steel. Blood overran the U-boat's wet deck, and sluiced down through the scuppers, darkly and agreeably red against the hated grey hull: she began to slide down, stern first, in a great upheaval of oil and air-bubbles and the smoke and smell of cordite. A man climbed half-way out of the conning-tower, throwing a weighted sack into the water as he did so: for a moment he wrestled to get his body clear, but the dead gunner must have jammed the escape-hatch, for the U-boat disappeared before he could free himself. A final explosion from below drove a cascade of oily water upwards: then there was silence. 'Cease fire' said Ericson, when the sea began to close in again and the surface flattened under a spreading film of oil. 'Wheel admidships. Stop engines. And stand by with those scrambling nets'.

The wonderful moment was over.

The Cruel Sea, Nicholas Monsarrat

* * *

Leaving a sinking ship. When leaving a sinking ship it is advisable to swim well clear as soon as possible to avoid air bubbles and wreckage which may rise to the surface with considerable force. If the ship is drifting it is better to leave her over the weather side, otherwise it may be difficult to swim clear of her. On the other hand oil fuel may extend for a considerable distance from the weather side of a drifting ship, and, whenever possible, oil fuel should be avoided, swimming below it if necessary to clear water. If you are unable to reach a boat or a raft, any floating wreckage will afford a temporary support.

If the ship has a list when you leave her, bear in mind that:

(i) if you leave her by the low side you may be struck by the masts, funnels or superstructure if the ship capsizes before you can swim clear;

(ii) jumping from the high side involves a risk of hitting the bilge keel or other projections such as the propellers, and if the under water part of the hull is exposed, barnacles may injure your feet and hands;

(iii) It is therefore preferable to leave by the bows or stern if possible.

The Naval Ratings Handbook, 1938 (British Admiralty)

Lifeboats at Aldeburgh.

What follows is a record of the extraordinary exchange of remarks between a woman and the lifeboatman who was trying to rescue her from a sinking ship. It happened towards the beginning of this century:

The great waves lifted the boat sometimes level with the rail of the ship, but as each wave passed the life-boat would drop fifteen to twenty feet down her side. The problem of getting the people to jump into the boat at the right moment was difficult in the extreme. Many of them jumped at the right moment and were safely stowed between the thwarts. The crew on the side nearest the ship would catch them as they jumped, while the five oarsmen on the further side manoeuvred with their oars to help in keeping the life-boat from crashing against the ship. My friend the carpenter on the side nearest the ship, who had caught a number of men as they jumped at the top of the wave, to his astonishment, as the boat rose for about the twentieth time, saw a handsome young lady dressed in black satin, with a baby in her arms with a white shawl and white bonnet, standing by the rail. Then this quaint conversation ensued: He shouted: 'Jump, ma'am'. But she had not time, nor did she seem ready to jump. As the boat disappeared he heard her voice saying: 'Am I to trust myself to you?'

The life-boat rose level with the deck again, and he said: 'Yes, ma'am, throw me the baby for a start'. She answered: 'No, I will stick to my baby. Can I trust you?'

But down went the boat again. A brief interval and my friend the carpenter showed his face at the deck level and shouted: 'I am a family man with two children. Come along, ma'am'. She replied with these astonishing words as the life-boat began another descent: 'Well, you look like a respectable man and I will trust you, but can you promise me we shan't get wet, with the baby's best clothes?' On the next reappearance of the life-boat it crashed against the side of the ship and our gallant carpenter grabbed the lady and baby and hauled them into the boat.

At that moment the boat was cut adrift and the sea caught her broadside-on. The next wave swept right over them, the lady in black satin and the baby held firmly in the arms of the carpenter. The lady said angrily, when the water had cleared away: 'I am sure you are a respectable man, but I don't know what you mean by letting a wave break right over my baby'.

Launch, Major-General Seely

Both mother and child survived and each year thereafter, for as long as anyone could remember, the woman wrote to the coxswain and every member of the crew, thanking them for saving her and her child.

* * *

Those who 'go down to the sea in ships' are exposed to unnatural stresses. The confined space, unpredictable elements, pitching and rolling of the ship and the unshakeable feeling of vulnerability and insignificance induce strange states of mind not experienced on land. In the

Opposite page. The lifeboats of Aldeburgh, on the east coast of England, have a long and honourable history. In front is the new James Cable lifeboat of the Rother class, 37-foot long and self-righting.

15th century, three-masted ships were able to hold a course closer to the wind than before and longer voyages could be planned with more certainty. But the psychological barriers remained:

There was a limit, moral rather than physical, to the length of a passage across open ocean without sight of land. Columbus in 1492 reached that limit with his 3000 miles passage from the Canaries to the Bahamas. He was a commander of strong personality, and yet he narrowly escaped a mutiny that would have cut short his voyage before he made his landfall. Neither he nor any other leader would have got a crew of those days to sail the 5000 miles that Toscanelli had stated as the westward distance to China. Toscanelli indeed had indicated Antillia and Cipango as refreshing places, but they were hearsay islands which no one had yet located. Columbus could get his attempt sanctioned only by making an unscientific reduction of the distance involved and by gaining the favour of Queen Isabella, whose mind, like his own, was mystical rather than mathematical.

The Cabot Voyages and Bristol Discovery under Henry VII, James A. Williamson

* * *

Although Joseph Conrad was born in the Ukraine of Polish parents, he wrote some of the best of all sea stories – in English. Conrad spent nearly twenty years as a sailor, including a spell gun-running for the Spanish royalists. He had an intimate relationship with ships and compassion and love for the men who sail in them. Here is his story of a rescue he carried out as a young man, which helped him later to write about the sea with so much sensitivity and understanding:

It had been a weirdly silent rescue – a rescue without a hail, without a single uttered word, without a gesture or a sign, without a conscious exchange of glances. Up to the very last moment those on board stuck to their pumps, which spouted two clear streams of water upon their bare feet. Their brown skin showed through the rents of their shirts; and the two small bunches of half-naked, tattered men went on bowing from the waist to each other in their back-breaking labour, up and down, absorbed, with no time for a glance over the shoulder at the help that was coming to them. As we dashed, unregarded, alongside a voice let out one, only one hoarse howl of command, and then, just as they stood, without caps, with the salt drying grey in the wrinkles and folds of their hairy, haggard faces, blinking stupidly at us their red eyelids, they made a bolt away from the handles, tottering and jostling against each other, and positively flung themselves over upon our very heads. The clatter they made tumbling into the boats had an extraordinarily destructive effect upon the illusion of tragic dignity our self-esteem had thrown over the contests of mankind with the sea. On that exquisite day of gentle breathing peace and veiled sunshine perished my romantic love to what

Opposite page. Naples. The busy port in the Bay of Naples, shown in hundreds of postcards, curving round to Vesuvius, with the island of Capri in the distance.

men's imagination had proclaimed the most august aspect of Nature. The cynical indifference of the sea to the merits of human suffering and courage, laid bare in this ridiculous, panic-tainted performance extorted from the dire extremity of nine good and honourable seamen revolted me. I saw the duplicity of the sea's most tender mood. It was so because it could not help itself but the awed respect of the early days was gone. I felt ready to smile bitterly at its enchanting charm and glare viciously at its furies. In a moment, before we shoved off, I had looked coolly at the life of my choice. Its illusions were gone, but its fascination remained. I had become a seaman at last.

Ordeal by Water, Joseph Conrad

Homeward Bound

Coming back home from the sea, for men, was returning to the welcoming arms of a woman: their wives, the women they loved, or a woman to spend the night with. The lives of sailors who embarked on faraway voyages were marked by long spells of chastity, so it was in the nature of things – and in the nature of young men – that the songs they sang were songs about women, the women they dreamt of at sea.

This is the verse of a sea shanty, sung in the 19th century in the fo'c's'les of British and American ships. *Acushla*, by the way, is a Gaelic word for sweetheart:

> We've courted gay Peruvian gals,
> French gals an' Chinee . . .
> Spanish gals an' Dutch gals too –
> And dainty Japanee.
> To far Australia, Honolulu too,
> Where the Hawaiian Maidens play.
> Just a different gal in every port,
> For that's the Sailor's way!
> Then it's goodbye, *acushla*,
> We're off to sea again.
> Sailor Jack – always comes back –
> To the gal he's left behind!

Once ashore, 'Jack', even before his seafaring rolling gait steadied down, went on the rampage – looking for a girl:

> So early in the morning,
> The Sailor likes the lasses, O! –
> ' The lasses o'Blythe and the lasses o'Shields,
> And the lasses across the water, O!

But ships do not stay in harbour for long and sailors have a 'love-'em-and-leave-'em' reputation. Women down the ages have been wary of their promises!

> O Shenandoah, I took a notion
> To sail across the stormy ocean.
> O Shenandoah, I'm bound to leave you . . .
> O Shenandoah, I'll not deceive you!

It has always been the way for women to wait and the men to go to sea. Even in the 1980s, when so many women have come from behind the kitchen sink and the sewing-machine, they still have to accept the waiting game:

Most seafarers are probably unaware that they are married to the ideal wife. Having swopped experiences with other wives in the same boat (to coin a phrase), I would like to draw the attention of seafaring husbands to the things that go on when they are away from home.

The ideal seafarer's wife is as faithful as a bloodhound, as independent as a long-distance runner, as practical as Barry Bucknell, and as well-adjusted as Lassie. She has to be. The difficulties she encounters during her husband's absences would send a lesser woman to a solicitor or a pychiatrist, or maybe to both.

First she has to convince herself that a conventional life is not necessarily the happiest one. To do this she has to cast off the deeply embedded idea that she should conform to what society thinks is 'normal' or usual – which means having a husband who, if not a completely nine-to-five man, is at least home for weekends, birthdays and Christmas and does not leave the happy matrimonial household for months at a time.

She is up against public opinion when she bravely looks on marriage to a seafarer as an advantage and not as a handicap. She endures that infuriating pity of her well-meaning friends with their nice safe, weekday-working husbands. 'I just don't know how you cope!', 'It isn't much of a life for you, is it?' From not-so-great friends there comes the subtle implication that anyone who calls that set-up a marriage must have been pretty hard up for a husband! Also lurking somewhere in the conversation is usually a question such as 'Don't you worry when he's so far away?', a question which every wife knows translates to 'Don't sailors still have a girl in every port?'

Jenny Penson, from *The Seaman's World* (selected by Ronald Hope)

* * *

The wives and girls they watch in the rain
For a ship as won't come home again.
'I reckon it's them head-winds,' they say,
'She'll be home tomorrow, if not today.
I'll just nip home 'n' I'll air the sheets
'N' buy the fixins 'n' cook the meats
As my man likes 'n' as my man eats'.
So home they goes by the windy streets,
Thinking their men are homeward bound
With anchors hungry for English ground,
And the bloody fun of it is, they're drowned!
Hear the yarn of a sailor,
An old yarn learned at sea.

The Yarn of the Loch Achray, John Masefield

* * *

Opposite page. Marseilles. A great Mediterranean port and the most important of all French ports. The second port of the town, the Vieux Port, is now kept for fishing boats and yachts.

The Remercie. An old Thames sailing barge moored at St Katharine's Dock, an historic part of the Port of London.

The wife of the lifeboat coxswain has a short wave radio in her front room, and stays tuned in to messages from the boat all the time they are out at sea . . . She pondered over whether to keep yet another hot dinner turning hard and dry in the oven, and finally threw away the pie and peas . . .

'I never touch his clothes when he's gone . . . And I never look out of the window to see them go — they say you see them for the last time'.

The Guardian, Polly Toynbee

* * *

Making fast, tying-up, after a night out at sea, is to breathe a sigh of relief. And when it has been a rough night, a sailor doesn't ask whom the moorings belong to!

Once — to be accurate, seventeen years ago — I had been out all night by myself in a boat called the *Silver Star*. She was a very small boat. She had only one sail) she was black inside and out, and I think about one hundred years old. I had hired her of a poor man, and she was his only possession.

It was a rough night in the late summer when the rich are compelled in their detestable grind to go to the Solent. When I say it was night I mean it was the early morning, just late enough for the rich to be asleep aboard their boats, and the dawn was silent upon the sea. There was a strong tide running up the Medina. I was tired to death. I had passed the Royal Yacht Squadron grounds, and the first thing I saw was a very fine and noble buoy — new-painted, gay, lordly — moorings worthy of a man!

I let go the halyard very briskly, and I nipped forward and got my hand upon that great buoy — there was no hauling of it inboard; I took the little painter of my boat and made it fast to this noble buoy, and then immediately I fell asleep. In this sleep of mine I heard, as in a pleasant dream, the exact motion of many oars rowed by strong men, and very soon afterwards I heard a voice with a Colonial accent swearing in an abominable manner, and I woke up and looked — and there was a man of prodigious wealth, all dressed in white, and with an extremely new cap on his head. His whiskers also were white and his face bright red, and he was in a great passion. He was evidently the owner or master of the buoy, and on either side of the fine boat in which he rowed were the rowers, his slaves. He could not conceive why I had tied the *Silver Star* to his magnificent great imperial moorings, to which he had decided to tie his own expensive ship, on which, no doubt, a dozen as rich as himself were sailing the seas.

I told him that I was sorry I had picked up his moorings, but that, in this country, it was the common courtesy of the sea to pick up any spare moorings one could find. I also asked him the name of his expensive ship, but he only answered with curses. I told him the name of my ship was the *Silver Star*.

Then, when I had cast off, I put out the sweeps and I rowed gently, for it was now slack water at the top of the tide, and I stood by while he tied his magnificent yacht to the

Opposite page. Port de Suffren, Paris. Built in 1896, the Belem is a three-masted barque, carrying 1,000 square metres of sail, and once used to transport cocoa from Brazil to France for Menier chocolate.

moorings. When he had done that I rowed under the stern of that ship and read her name. But I will not print it here, only let me tell you it was the name of a ship belonging to a fabulously rich man. Riches, I thought then and I think still, corrupt the heart.

This and That and the Other, Hilaire Belloc

* * *

The British marine artist Norman Wilkinson tells the story of a trawler on naval service during 1915, whose skipper had brought her from the eastern Mediterranean to Malta:

'You got your Admiralty charts before leaving?' inquired an officer. 'No Sir, we got no Admiralty charts'. 'Good god, man how did you get through the Greek islands?' 'Well, Sir, the Mate had an old Bible with some quite good maps at the end'.

A History of Seamanship, Douglas Phillips-Birt

* * *

The Bayou Boeuf opened into the estuary of the Atchafalaya River, and Morgan City was a ramshackle patchwork of low roofs squatting on the junction. I cruised along its beach looking for a place to land. On the edge of the estuary there was a fisherman's jetty with two jonboats moored up to its few remaining piles. I grounded on soft mud, and was met by an old man trailing a line of catfish hooks.

'What you want?'

'I wondered if I could tie up here for the night –'

'You could lose your boat. Nothing's safe in this town'.

'Why's that?'

'*Lot* of drifters about'.

He took in my scuffed cases with a glance of scornful recognition.

'Oh. Why do *they* come here?'

'Looking for work'. He looked at me again and gave an amused snort. 'They don't get none, though. It'll cost you a dollar –'

'Fine.'

'In advance'.

Old Glory, Jonathan Raban

* * *

There are times when any hope of returning home has gone and is only rekindled when a lifeboat heaves in sight. The story that comes now is a true epic of the sea, told personally by the mate of the *Indian Chief* to Clark Russell, who wrote it for the *Daily Telegraph* long ago:

Of a sudden I took it into my head to fancy that the mizen-mast wasn't so secure as the fore-mast. It came into my mind like a fright, and I sang out to the captain that I meant to make for the fore-top. I don't know whether he heard me or made any answer. Maybe it was a sort of craze of mine for the moment, but I was wild to leave that mast as soon as ever I began to fear for it. I cast my lashings adrift, and gave a look at the deck and saw that I mustn't go that way if I did not want to be drowned. So I climbed into the crosstrees and swung myself on to the stay, working down to the main-top, and so to the main crosstrees; then hand over hand down the topmast-stay to the fore-top. If I had stopped to reflect before leaving the mizen-top, I should not have believed I had the strength to work my way forward like that; my hands felt as if they'd been skinned, and my finger-joints seemed to have no use in them.

There were nine or ten men in the fore-top, all lashed and huddled together. The mast rocked badly, and the throbbing of it to the thrashing of the great tatters of canvas gave a horrible sensation. There was not a man but thought his time was come, and though death seemed terrible when I looked down on the boiling waters below, yet the pain of the cold almost killed the craving for life.

It was now about three o'clock on Thursday morning; the air was full of the strange, dim light of the foam and the stars, and I could plainly see the black swarm of men in the mizen-top and rigging. I was looking that way when a great sea fell upon the hull of the ship with a fearful crash. A moment after, the main-mast went. It fell quickly, and as it fell it bore down the mizen-mast. There was a horrible noise of splintering wood, and some piercing cries; and then another great sea swept over the after-deck; and we who were looking from the foretop saw the stumps of the two masts sticking up from the bottom of the hold, the mizen-mast slanting over the bulwarks into the water, with the men lashed to it drowning. There never was a more shocking sight, and the wonder is that some who saw it did not go raving mad. The fore-mast still stood, complete to the royals, and all the yards in place. But every instant I expected to find myself heaving through the air.

By this time the ship was completely gutted, the upper part of her just a frame of ribs; and the gale still blew furiously. Indeed, I gave up hope when the mizen fell and I saw my shipmates drowning on it.

It must have been half an hour after this that a man who was jammed close against me pointed out into the dark, and cried in a wild, hoarse voice, 'Isn't that a steamer's light?' I looked, but, what with grief and suffering and cold, I was nearly blind, and could see nothing. Presently another man sang out that he could see a light; and this was echoed by another; so I told them to keep their eyes open and watch if it moved. By and by they said it was stationary; but though we couldn't guess that it meant anything good for us, yet this light heaving in sight, and our talk of it gave us some comfort.

When the dawn broke we saw the smoke of a steamer, and agreed it was her light we had seen; but I made nothing of that smoke, and was looking heartbrokenly at the mizen-mast and the cluster of drowned men washing about it, when a loud cry made me turn my head, and then I saw a lifeboat under a reefed foresail heading direct for us. It was a sight, sir, to make one crazy with joy; and it put the strength of ten men into every one of us.

The Daily Telegraph, 11 January 1881

* * *

Ships' bells were struck at intervals to sound out the time and to mark the end of 'watches', the periods of duty on board that last four hours, except for the 'dog watches' which are two hours (1600 to 1800 and 1800 to 2000 hours). At the end of a 'watch' the sailors who had been on duty could go to their bunks and rest, but if conditions were rough, they would have to stay on deck to help out.

The words of *Strike the Bell*, are a cry from the heart of tired seamen on British and American sailing ships, in the later half of the 19th century:

> Aft on the poop deck and walking about,
> There's the second mate, so steady and so stout.
> What he is a-thinking of he doesn't know himsel':
> We wish that he would hurry up and strike, strike the bell.
>
> Strike the bell, second mate, let us go below;
> Look well to wind'ard, you can see it's going to blow.
> Look at the glass, you can see that in a spell;
> We wish that you would hurry up and strike, strike the bell.
>
> Down on the main deck and working at the pumps,
> There's the starboard watch all a-longing for their bunks;
> Looking out to wind'ard they see a great swell:
> They're wishing that the second mate would strike, strike the bell.
>
> Aft at the wheel poor Anderson stand,
> Grasping at the wheel with his cold, mittened hands;
> Looking at the compass, oh, the course is clear as hell:
> He's wishing that the second mate would strike, strike the bell.
>
> For'ard on the fo'c's'le head a-keeping sharp lookout,
> Young Johnny's standing, ready for to shout:
> 'Lights are burning bright, sir, and everything is well.'
> He's wishing that the second mate would strike, strike the bell.
>
> Aft on the quarterdeck the gallant captain stands,
> Looking out to wind'ard with a spy-glass in his hands;
> What he is a-thinking of we know very well:
> He's thinking more of shortening sail than striking the bell.
>
> *Strike the Bell*, selected by Roy Palmer

* * *

Making a landfall, especially when you are tired, is not always straightforward and most sailors have had the humiliating experience of not recognising a familiar headland or stretch of coast. If that has ever happened to you, you are in good company. Writer, poet and gentleman-sailor, Hilaire Belloc, recalls how he was fooled:

One would think that the outline of the headland, once one had known it from a particular side, was an unmistakable thing, and one would think that the same would be true of a characteristic range of hills seen lengthwise, or even of the entrance to a valley harbour.

After all, the same sort of thing is at once recognisable by land: a man does not mistake the Wrekin, or the Malvern Hills.

But at sea, for some mysterious reason, you never can be sure; and that is why such pains are taken in the elaborate descriptions and plans of sailing directions, and in the little pictures which they make in the official books. It is not only a matter of what is called to-day 'visibility', though it is true that the thickness of the air makes a great difference to one's judgment of distance. No matter what the conditions, the most absurd mistakes can be made, and are made continually, and that by practised men. It was only the other day that I mistook Grisnez for the end of the cliff some miles to the east of it above the flat of Calais. You would think that Beachy Head, seen from up-Channel looking westward, was unmistakable; for it has the exact outline of a hippopotamus, with its little ear and fat forehead and snout, and there is a long flat before it, so that anything rising up, one would think, was bound to be Beachy Head, but it is not so. A man who has been knocking about the Channel at night, and does not quite know where he is, except that he is somewhere off the Sussex coast, may (it sounds absurd, but it is true) take Fairlight in a haze for Beachy Head, or (coming eastwards) he may catch in a dull dawn the low cliffs beyond Newhaven, and, if the thick air hides Beachy Head from him, he may take these for that headland.

The Cruise of the Nona, Hilaire Belloc

* * *

Coming into port in the pre-jet-age days of the great ocean-going liners was an *occasion*, leisurely, gracious, important, something altogether different from landing at Heathrow or Kennedy Airport. Alistair Cooke sighs for what we have lost:

In Memoriam: The Ship's Reporter

There used to be a special job on the New York newspapers which was hotly competed for by young reporters – the job of *ship's reporter*. If you were lucky enough to get it, your daily routine started by turning to the shipping section of the *New York Times* in which, in those days, one whole page of eight columns was often not enough to keep tabs on the enormous bustle of passenger ships coming and going from the berths on the Hudson River. And the shipping companies provided the papers with manifests or, at least, a list of incoming passengers who aspired to some sort of fame. The reporter then picked out the ship and the celebrity he wanted to interview, made a note of the tide-tables, called the Coastguards to find out when the press cutter would be off down the bay and, an hour or more before high tide – quite often at dawn – joined a little band of other ship's reporters and newsreel cameramen and sailed off down the river to the narrows, and boarded the liner when it stopped for immigration.

Nowadays the shipping news is relegated to about an eighth of a column, and there will be nothing out of Manhattan. You can stand at twilight on top of the Empire State Building and look across to the docks in the West Forties and see the empty slots of the berths – like the

Genoa. Italy's chief Mediterranean port, in the Gulf of Genoa, and a ship-building centre since the Middle Ages.

teeth of some beached whale – where once, in the first weeks of September, you would have seen a continuous rank of liners and smoking funnels. I've been up there and seen a noble parade of the *Normandie*, the *Europa*, one of the *Queens*, the *Olympic*, the *United States*, the *Leonardo da Vinci* and a dozen more – now in the jet-age, all gone. And with them the trade – the art – of the ship's reporter.

Alistair Cooke, *Letter from America*

* * *

William James Slade made his first voyage when only a few months old, taken to sea by his mother on his father's small coastal sailing ship. He became a British coastal seaman himself, and later a shipmaster and shipowner. He looks back on his long life as a master mariner:

Well, now I feel it is time I closed this rather rough and, perhaps, garbled account of the life of a coastal sailor. Sometimes it was hard to endure and, of course, in summertime it was often a pleasure. There were times when life became almost intolerable, but compensation for this could always be found. It took us away from home for long periods, often months, but seafaring men learned to appreciate the saying that 'Absence makes the heart grow fonder' more than the average person. If I were asked the question: 'Do you regret your life on the sea?' I would, after careful thought, say, 'To be born as I was in a seafaring community of a seafaring family, in those days, there was nothing better I could have done'. For practically forty years I was seasick, but during all the years of my manhood I never allowed this to get me down. I was always ready to face another bout of this miserable affliction. I wonder sometimes if it wasn't really a blessing in disguise. Although getting on in years I have yet to face the first illness due, perhaps, to having my system cleared of its impurities. I have often regretted my inability to get away to a deepwater life. Yes, I think I would have gone to the top in that sphere of life and probably spent many years as master in a deepwater ship, but would this have been a more remunerative or comfortable existence? I have great doubts. For one thing I was my own master for the big majority of those years at sea, responsible to no one, a freedom that could not exist in any other branch of sea life.

Out of Appledore, W. J. Slade

* * *

We'll Go to Sea
No More

I never liked the landsman's life,
   The earth is aye the same;
Give me the ocean for my dower,
   My vessel for my hame.
Give me the fields that no man ploughs,

Opposite page. Porto Empedocle. The main harbour on the south west coast of Sicily, serving Agrigento which the Greeks founded in 582BC, and the point of embarkation for the Pelagian islands to the south.

Agios Nikolaos. In the heart of Mirabelo Bay, this is journey's end for many fishing boats on the north east coast of Crete, the largest of the Greek islands.

The farm that pays no fee:
Give me the bonny fish that glance
So gladly through the sea.
When life's last sun goes feebly down,
And death comes to our door,
When all the world's a dream to us,
We'll go to sea no more.
from a Scottish folk poem in *The Sea, Ships and Sailors* (selected by
William Cole)

* * *

The time comes for ships and books to reach their journey's end. Hilaire Belloc had owned a succession of small ships, modest vessels mostly, but they were all dear to him. They were his friends and, to use an old-fashioned word now, his mistresses. About the *Nona*, his best-loved boat of all, he once said 'We are nearly of an age, the darling, but she a little younger, as is fitting'. But whatever their age, ships do not always live as long as their masters:

The other day there was *a ship that died*. It was my own ship, and in a way I would it had not died. But die it had to, for it was mortal, having been made in this world: to be accurate, at Bembridge, in the Isle of Wight, nearly sixty years ago. Moreover, since boats also must die, it is right that they should die their own death in their own element; not violently, but after due preparation; for, in spite of modern cowardice, it is better to be prepared for death than unprepared. . .

She had been patched up for years past. So are men in their old age and their decay. As the years proceeded she had been more and more patched up. So are men more and more patched up as the years proceed. Yet all those who loved her tried to keep her going to the very last. So it is with men.

But my boat was happier than men in this, that no one desired her death. She had nothing to leave, except an excellent strong memory of days calm, days windy, days peerless, days terrific, days humorous, days empty in long flats without a breath of wind, days beckoning, principally in the early mornings, leading on her admirable shape, empress of harbours and of the narrow seas. Also, she had no enemies, and no one feared her. There was no one to say, as there is of men, 'I shall be glad when they are out of the way'. There was no one to wish her that very evil wish which some men do other men – themselves evil: 'I am glad to think that he is dead'.

No. My boat went most honourably and straightly to her death. She had nothing to repent, nothing to regret, nothing to fear, nothing to be the cause of shame. It is so with things inanimate, and, indeed, with animals. It is so with everything upon this earth except man.

A Conversation with a Cat and Others, Hilaire Belloc

* * *

Hodder & Stoughton Limited: *Gipsy Moth Circles the World* by Francis Chichester. Reprinted by permission of Hodder & Stoughton Limited and John Farquharson Limited.

Chapter 3 – *High and Dry*
The Observer: *The Champagne Boat People* by Alan Road.
Hutchinson Publishing Group Limited: *Ship Shape* by Olive Cook and *Sea Days, Sea Flowers* by H. E. Bates (*The Saturday Book*).
Angus & Robertson (UK) Ltd.: *The Circumnavigators* by Donald Holm.
The Circumnavigators by Donald Holm © 1974 by Donald R. Holm. Reprinted by permission of the publisher Prentice-Hall, Inc., Englewood Cliffs, NJ 07632.
George Allen & Unwin Publishers Ltd.: *The Ra Expeditions* by Thor Heyerdahl.
Excerpts from *The Ra Expeditions* by Thor Heyerdahl. English translation Copyright © 1971 by George Allen & Unwin Ltd. Translation from the Norwegian Copyright © 1970 by Thor Heyerdahl. Reprinted by permission of Doubleday & Company, Inc.
Cecil Lewis: *Turn Right for Corfu* (published by Hutchinson & Co. (Publishers) Ltd.).
Arthur Barker Limited: *Famous Rescues at Sea* by Richard Garrett.
Gerald Duckworth & Company Ltd.: *When the Going Was Good* by Evelyn Waugh.
When the Going Was Good by Evelyn Waugh © 1962 by Evelyn Waugh, by permission of Little, Brown and Company.

Chapter 4 – *Ol' Man River*
Chappell Music Ltd.: *Ol' Man River* by Jerome Kern/Oscar Hammerstein II copyright: 1927 T. B. Harms Co. U.K. Publisher: Chappell Music Limited. Reproduced by kind permission.
Ol' Man River written by Jerome Kern and Oscar Hammerstein, II © 1927 T. B. Harms Company copyright renewed. (c/o The Welk Music Group, Santa Monica, CA 90401). International copyright secured. All rights reserved. Used by permission.
William Collins Sons & Co. Ltd.: *Old Glory* by Jonathan Raban. Simon & Schuster, New York: Copyright 1981 by Jonathan Raban. Reprinted by permission of Simon & Schuster.
Hutchinson Publishing Group Limited: *The Oxford & Cambridge Boat Race* by Christopher Dodd and *Henley Royal Regatta* by Christopher Dodd.
Faber & Faber (Publishers) Ltd.: *Venice* by James Morris and *Travels* by James Morris. Reprinted by permission of the author.
David & Charles: *Spritsail Barges of Thames and Medway* by Edgar J. March and *Bradshaw's Canals and Navigable Rivers of England and Wales* compiled by Henry Rodolph de Salis.
Passages from *The Narrow Boat* by Tom Chaplin are reprinted by kind permission of the author and the publishers, Whittet Books Ltd., 113 Westbourne Grove, W2 4UP.

Chapter 5 – *Business in Great Waters*
Faber & Faber Publishers: *The Great Port – A Passage Through New York* by Jan Morris. Reprinted by permission of the author.
Victor Gollancz Ltd.: *An Orkney Tapestry* by George Mackay Brown.
George Allen & Unwin Publishers Ltd.: *The Kon-Tiki Expedition* by Thor Heyerdahl.
From *Kon-Tiki*, by Thor Heyerdahl. © 1985, 1978, 1950 by Thor Heyerdahl. Published in the United States by Rand McNally & Company.
A. D. Peters & Co. Ltd.: *Hills and the Sea* by Hilaire Belloc (published by Methuen & Co. Ltd.) and

Midshipman Hornblower by C. S. Forester (published by Michael Joseph).
Mr. Midshipman Hornblower by C. S. Forester © 1950 by C. S. Forester by permission of Little, Brown and Company.
The Guardian: article by J. R. L. Anderson.
B. T. Batsford Limited: *Paddle Steamers* by Richard Clammer.
Cassell & Co. Ltd.: *The War Speeches of the Rt. Hon. Winston S. Churchill* compiled by Charles Eade.
Sir Peter Scott for permission to quote from *The Battle of the Narrow Seas* (published by Country Life Ltd. and White Lion Publishers).
Campbell Thomson & McLaughlin Limited: *The Cruel Sea* by Nicholas Monsarrat (published by Cassell Ltd.), with the permission of Mrs. Ann Monsarrat.
Alfred A. Knopf, Inc.: *The Cruel Sea* by Nicholas Monsarrat. Copyright Nicholas Monsarrat, 1951.
Hodder & Stoughton Limited: *Launch* by Major-General J. E. B. Seely, with acknowledgement to the author's Executors.
Hakluyt Society: *The Cabot Voyages and Bristol Discovery under Henry VII* by James A. Williamson (published by Cambridge University Press).

Chapter 6 – *Homeward Bound*
Hutchinson Publishing Group Limited: *The Sailor's Way* from *Sea Shanties* by Stan Hugill.
Harrap Limited: *The Seaman's World* edited by Ronald Hope, with acknowledgements to The Marine Society and Mrs. Jenny Penson.
The Society of Authors, literary representative of the Estate of John Masefield: *The Yarn of the Loch Achray*.
Macmillan Publishing Company, New York: *The Yarn of the Loch Achray* from *Poems of John Masefield*, copyright 1953.
Polly Toynbee for permission to quote from her article in *The Guardian*.
A. D. Peters & Co. Ltd.: *This and That and the Other* by Hilaire Belloc (published by Methuen & Co. Ltd.).
Topic Records: for the words of *Strike the Bell* (printed in *Strike the Bell*, selected by Roy Palmer, published by Cambridge University Press).
Century Publishing Co. Ltd. and Hippocrene Books Inc.: *The Cruise of the Nona* by Hilaire Belloc.
BBC and *The Listener*: *Letter from America* by Alistair Cooke.
Rupert Hart Davis: *The Sea, Ships and Sailors* by William Cole.
Viking Penguin Inc.: extract from *The Sea, Ships and Sailors* by William Cole. Copyright © 1967 by William Cole. Reprinted by permission of Viking Penguin Inc.
Macmillan Publishing Company, New York: *A Conversation with a Cat and Others* by Hilaire Belloc. Copyright 1931 Hilaire Belloc. Published by Cassell & Co Ltd. Reprinted by permission of Macmillan Publishing Company.
A. D. Peters & Co. Ltd.: *A Conversation with a Cat and Others* by Hilaire Belloc.

We should also like to thank the following for lending us rare books and for help in other ways: Mr. William Burrell (Coxswain of the Aldeburgh Lifeboats), Mr. F. X. Kay, Mr. Dermod MacCarthy (who crewed for Hilaire Belloc) and Mrs. Daphne Staveley. And we single out for special thanks: Mrinalini Srivastava for all her care in editing and designing the book, Susie Saunders for indefatigably seeking permission to use copyright material and Malcolm Saunders for encouragement and support right from the beginning.